Concis

Bird

Guide

There are 47 individual Wildlife Trusts covering the whole of the UK and the Isle of Man and Alderney. Together The Wildlife Trusts are the largest UK voluntary organization dedicated to protecting wildlife and wild places everywhere – at land and sea. They are supported by 791,000 members, 150,000 of whom belong to their junior branch, Wildlife Watch. Every year The Wildlife Trusts work with thousands of schools, and their nature reserves and visitor centres receive millions of visitors.

The Wildlife Trusts work in partnership with hundreds of landowners and businesses in the UK. Building on their existing network of 2,250 nature reserves, The Wildlife Trusts' recovery plan for the UK's wildlife and fragmented habitats, known as A Living Landscape, is being achieved through restoring, recreating and reconnecting large areas of wildlife habitat.

The Wildlife Trusts also have a vision for the UK's seas and sea life – Living Seas, in which wildlife thrives from the depths of the oceans to the coastal shallows. In Living Seas, wildlife and habitats are recovering, the natural environment is adapting well to a changing climate, and people are inspired by marine wildlife and value the sea for the many ways in which it supports our quality of life. As well as protecting wildlife, these projects help to safeguard the ecosystems we depend on for services like clean air and water.

All 47 Wildlife Trusts are members of the Royal Society of Wildlife Trusts (Registered charity number 207238). To find your local Wildlife Trust visit wildlifetrusts.org

THE
wildlife
TRUSTS

Concise
Bird
Guide

NEW
HOLLAND

Third reprint 2011
First published in 2010 by New Holland Publishers (UK) Ltd
London · Cape Town · Sydney · Auckland
www.newhollandpublishers.com
Garfield House, 86–88 Edgware Road, London W2 2EA, UK
80 McKenzie Street, Cape Town 8001, South Africa
Unit 1, 66 Gibbes Street, Chatswood, New South Wales 2067, Australia
218 Lake Road, Northcote, Auckland, New Zealand
Reprinted with revisions 2011

10 9 8 7 6 5 4 3

ISBN 978 1 84773 601 7

Series Editor: Krystyna Mayer
Design: Alan Marshall
Artwork: Richard Allen, Dan Cole, David Daly, Szabolcs Kokay & Stephen Message
Production: Melanie Dowland
Publisher: Simon Papps

The publishers thank Michael Allen of The Wildlife Trusts for reading the text.

Reproduction by Modern Age Repro Co. Ltd., Hong Kong
Printed and bound in China by Leo Paper Group

Other titles in series
Concise Butterfly & Moth Guide
Concise Wild Flower Guide
Concise Insect Guide

Concise Tree Guide
Concise Garden Wildlife Guide

Contents

Introduction

Birds are probably the most familiar class of animal in Britain and Ireland. Of the world's 10,000 or so species about 420 breed in Europe, and of these over 200 species regularly breed in Britain and Ireland.

Recognizing Birds

This handy and portable book provides basic practical information, including variations in plumage colours, to enable quick identification of species in the field. The size of each species is given in average lengths. As you become more experienced you will be able to recognize some species very quickly and at a distance. Recognizing birds involves answering a number of questions. How does it fly? What is its shape? Are there any distinguishing characteristics, such as the shape of the bill, the length of the tail or the length of the legs? What are the colours? Are there any characteristic plumage patterns? How does the bird behave? What noise does it make? Where is it? The answers to all these questions will help you to identify the species to which a bird belongs.

The flight of species or groups of birds can be a major clue to their identity. Woodland birds such as woodpeckers have a distinctly undulating flight, which is particularly noticeable when they are flying across an open area. Kingfishers have a fast and direct flight often close to the surface of water. The shape in flight may also be distinctive: ducks have pointed wings that move rapidly and necks that are outstretched.

Colour is not always a good guide, because the quality of light and the effect of local colour can cause variations that no book can cater for. The patterns of the plumage are probably more important. Note that the plumage of birds can vary at different times of the year and at intermediate stages, for example between juveniles and non-breeding birds.

Behaviour of birds differs between species. Ducks, for example, can be divided into two groups depending on their feeding behaviour. One group dives beneath the surface to feed, while the other feeds from the surface. Many species are likely to be seen in flocks, while others are generally seen singly. Some, such as Bullfinches, are frequently seen in pairs. To assist in recognition, look at the way a bird is feeding and relating to other birds.

The songs, calls and other noises that birds make are obvious, if difficult identification characteristics. Everyone is familiar with the call of the male Cuckoo, a bird more often heard than seen, but how many of us can recognize the bubbling call of the female? The call of the Kingfisher may be the first clue to its presence, and the skulking Nightingale is recognized more frequently by its song than visually.

The best way to build your identification skills is to become familiar with the birds you see or hear often. This will give you a series of yardsticks with which to compare other species. Build up your portfolio of species, and if you cannot identify a bird you may still be able to identify the group to which it belongs.

Bird Topography

The illustration of a female Reed Bunting below shows some of the key terms used to describe the main features of birds.

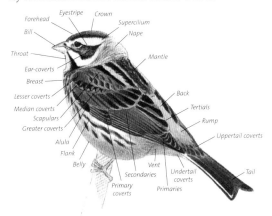

Mute Swan
Cygnus olor

SIZE AND DESCRIPTION 152cm. Largest flying bird in Britain. Adult is all white, juvenile grey-brown. Distinguished from wintering Bewick's and Whooper Swans by orange bill with black knob at base (smaller in female) and more graceful curve to neck.

VOICE Generally silent; hisses when angry or disturbed.

HABITAT Almost any still or slow-moving inland water body; also estuaries and sheltered coastal regions. Found across northern and western Europe. Resident in Britain.

FOOD AND HABITS Usually feeds on water by dipping its neck below the surface, sometimes up-ending. Nest a large mound of plant matter on the edges of water bodies.

Adult

Juvenile

Bewick's Swan *Cygnus columbianus*

Whooper Swan *Cygnus cygnus*

SIZE AND DESCRIPTION
Bewick's 125cm;
Whooper 150cm.
Bewick's has a
slightly shorter and
thicker neck, and a
neater bill with the
yellow area smaller
and rounder than in
Whooper. In the
latter, the shape of
the yellow on the
bill is more pointed
and extends further
towards the bill tip.

Bewick's Swan adult

Bewick's Swan juvenile

Whooper Swan juvenile

Whooper Swan adult

VOICE Whooper
makes bugle-like
whooping calls.
Bewick's calls are shorter and less echoing.

HABITAT Bewick's breeds on lakes on the Russian arctic tundra,
wintering on wet meadows in the Low Countries and Britain.
Whooper breeds on north European lakes, and winters on meadows,
fields and wetlands in central and western Europe, and the Black Sea.

FOOD AND HABITS Mainly feeds on aquatic plants and grasses; in winter
also grain and vegetables from fields. Nest a large mound of plant
matter on small islands or the edges of water bodies.

Brent Goose *Branta bernicla*

Barnacle Goose *Branta leucopsis*

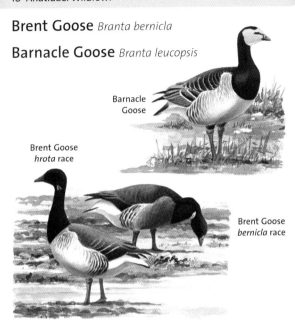

Barnacle
Goose

Brent Goose
hrota race

Brent Goose
bernicla race

SIZE AND DESCRIPTION Brent 60cm; Barnacle 65cm. Small and neat dark geese with stubby bills and black necks. Brent has an all-black head, Barnacle a pale face. Two races of Brent occur in Britain: Light-bellied (*B. b. hrota*) on the west coast and in Ireland, and Dark-bellied (*B. b. bernicla*) in the east and south.

VOICE Brent makes a subdued 'rrott', Barnacle a barking 'kak'.

HABITAT Breed in northern Europe; winter in north-west Europe.

FOOD AND HABITS Brent feeds on intertidal eelgrasses and other vegetation. Barnacle eats mainly grass.

Canada Goose
Branta canadensis

SIZE AND DESCRIPTION 97cm. A large grey-brown goose with a black head and neck, and a white patch on the chin that extends up the head. Distinguished from Barnacle and Brent Geese by larger size, longer neck and preference for inland habitats.

VOICE Loud trumpet-like call, 'ah-honk'.

HABITAT Inland waters including park lakes and ponds; also coasts and marshes during winter. Introduced to Britain and now common and widespread; also some vagrants from North America.

FOOD AND HABITS Feeds mainly on grass. Nest a down-lined cup, usually near water.

Canada Goose

Barnacle Goose

Brent Goose

Greylag Goose
Anser anser

SIZE AND DESCRIPTION 83cm. Large grey goose with an orange bill and flesh-coloured legs.

VOICE Calls in flight 'aahng-ung-ung'.

HABITAT Marshy moorland during breeding season. Winter visitor to salt-water and freshwater marshes, grasslands and estuaries. Feral birds present in Britain throughout the year, but wild birds are mostly winter visitors.

FOOD AND HABITS Diet mostly grass, but also cereals in autumn and winter. Nest a down-lined cup on the ground.

Pink-footed Goose
Anser brachyrhynchus

SIZE AND DESCRIPTION 70cm. Small and neat grey goose with a rounded head and short neck that are darker than the rest of its body. The legs are pink, and there is a pink band on the bill.

VOICE Vocal; call a ringing 'ung unk' and 'wink wink wink'.

HABITAT Breeds in Iceland and Spitsbergen. Winters on coastal meadows in Britain and the Low Countries. In Britain found predominantly in Norfolk, Lancashire and eastern Scotland).

FOOD AND HABITS Diet is almost entirely vegetarian.

▶ **SIMILAR SPECIES Bean Goose** (*A. fabalis*). 75cm long. Orange legs, narrow orange band on bill and darker plumage than that of Pink-footed Goose. Breeds in north-east Europe and Siberia; winters in coastal wetlands in north-west Europe. Scarce in Britain; mainly on east coast.

White-fronted Goose
Anser albifrons

Juvenile

Adult

SIZE AND DESCRIPTION 70cm. Two races appear in large wintering flocks in Britain. Greenland White-fronts (*A. a. flavirostris*) winter in Ireland and Scotland, smaller Russian birds (*A. a. albifrons*) in Wales and southern England. Greenland birds have orange bills and legs, Russian ones pink bills and orange legs. Adult of both races has a white forehead and black belly markings.

VOICE Call higher pitched than that of other grey geese, and with a whinnying quality.

HABITAT Breeds on tundra. Winters on rough grassland, salt-water and freshwater marshes, and fields.

FOOD AND HABITS Feeds on herbs, grasses and sedges, as well as agricultural grain, potatoes and sprouting cereals (the latter particularly in winter).

Mandarin Duck *Aix galericulata*

Female

Male

Female

Juvenile

Length 45cm. Male in breeding plumage is a vivid mixture of clearly defined orange, green, white and other colours. Female is grey-brown with spots on the flanks and a fine stripe behind a white eyering. Naturalized species originating in the Far East. Found throughout Britain in small numbers; increasingly common in south. Feeds on plant matter, insects, worms and small aquatic animals; partial to acorns. Breeds in holes in mature trees. Threatened in original habitat, so European populations are of conservation significance.

Egyptian Goose *Alopochen aegyptiaca*

Length 70cm. Sexes are alike. Variations in plumage, from light to dark, not sex or age related. An African species introduced to north-west Europe, with Britain, the Netherlands and Germany having self-sustaining populations. Found in rivers, lakes and ponds in parks. Uncommon in Britain, but increasing in south-east. Feeds on plant matter; also sometimes small animals. Often nests in holes in mature trees.

Shelduck
Tadorna tadorna

Juvenile

Female

Male

Size and description 61cm. Large duck with bold markings: head and neck dark green, wide chestnut breast band, black on wingtips and end of tail, and white underparts. Sexes are similar.

Voice Generally silent, but drake can give a whistle when in flight. Female quacks.

Habitat Estuaries, sandy shores and salt marshes. Breeds mainly on coasts, and occasionally also on rivers and lakes.

Food and habits Feeds chiefly on small molluscs caught by sweeping bill through soft estuarine mud. Nests in dunes in rabbit burrows.

Mallard
Anas platyrhynchos

Female

Male

SIZE AND DESCRIPTION 58cm. Britain's most common duck. Drake has a dark rich brown breast, and a dark green head with a white collar in breeding season. Speculum (a bright, often iridescent patch of colour on the wings of some birds, especially ducks) is purple.

VOICE Ducks give the familiar 'quack'; drake has a higher-pitched call.

HABITAT Resident and widespread throughout Europe, occurring on almost any inland waters other than fast-flowing rivers. Often more coastal in winter.

FOOD AND HABITS Surface feeding, it can be seen dabbling and up-ending. Eats a variety of food, including invertebrates, fish and plants. Usually nests on the ground under bushes, close to water.

Gadwall
Anas strepera

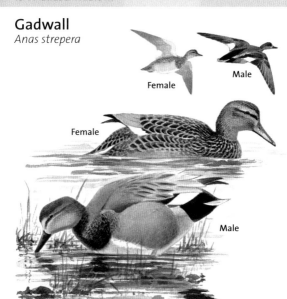

Female

Male

Female

Male

Size and description 51cm. Male grey with a blackish rump and bill. Female similar to female Mallard, but smaller. Both sexes have a characteristic white speculum. Legs are orange-yellow.

Voice A wooden 'errp'.

Habitat Mainly inland waters, and occasionally coastal marshes or estuaries. Present in Britain throughout the year, but rarely breeds.

Food and habits Diet consists of seeds, leaves, roots and stems of aquatic plants, as well as grasses and stoneworts; occasionally also cereal grains on land. Not as gregarious as some other dabbling ducks outside breeding season, tending to form only small flocks.

Wigeon
Anas penelope

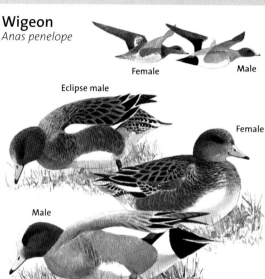

Female

Male

Eclipse male

Female

Male

SIZE AND DESCRIPTION 18cm. Drake has a chestnut head with a creamy yellow stripe from the bill over the crown, pinkish breast and short black-tipped blue bill. Speculum is green. White patches on the wings are visible in flight.

VOICE Drake has a whistling 'whee-oo' call.

HABITAT Marshes. Breeds in north. Winter visitor to much of central and southern Europe, including Britain, often on coastal marshes and estuaries, but also inland.

FOOD AND HABITS Eats mostly plant matter, which it takes from the water's surface. Often seen in flocks grazing on land.

Common Teal
Anas crecca

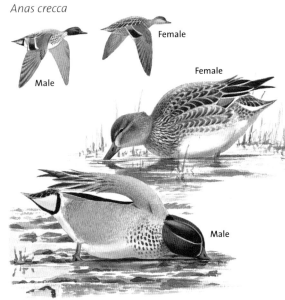

Male

Female

Female

Male

Male

Size and description 35cm. Smaller and neater in appearance than Mallard. Drake has a chestnut head with a green eyestripe, speckled breast and creamy undertail. Speculum is green.

Voice Drake gives a whistling 'crrick, crrick' call.

Habitat Prefers still or slow-moving fresh water with dense fringing vegetation. Resident in much of Europe.

Food and habits A dabbling duck, eating mostly plants and seeds. May nest some distance from water. Fast in flight; springs up from water.

Shoveler
Anas clypeata

Male

Female

Female

Eclipse male

Male

SIZE AND DESCRIPTION 51cm. Surface-feeding duck easily recognized by its very large spatulate bill. Drake has a dark green head, white breast and chestnut flanks. Forewing is blue. Speculum is green.

VOICE Drake calls 'took-took'; females 'quack'.

HABITAT Lakes and reservoirs; favours creeks, reed beds and marshy areas with plenty of cover. Summer visitor to northern and eastern Europe, year-round resident in western Europe and winter visitor to southern Europe.

FOOD AND HABITS Feeds in shallow muddy water; sieves seeds through bill. Nest a down-lined grass cup well hidden on the ground.

Pintail
Anas acuta

SIZE AND DESCRIPTION Female 56cm; male 66cm. Elegant male has a black tail, chocolate head and pure white breast. Female has a slim neck, dark bill, short pointed tail and overall brownish plumage.

VOICE Rarely vocal; drake has a low whistle, female a low quack and churring growl.

HABITAT Breeds on moors and freshwater marshes in north-east Europe. Winters on sheltered coastal waters and sometimes inland in southern and western Europe.

FOOD AND HABITS Dabbles and upends in shallow water. Winter diet includes aquatic plants, and roots, grains and other seeds. During nesting season eats mainly invertebrate animals. Gregarious, forming flocks with other ducks outside breeding season.

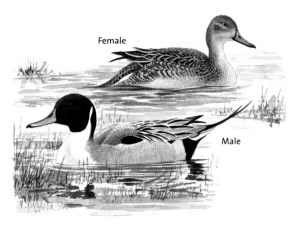

Female

Male

Garganey *Anas querquedula*

Length 40cm. A dabbling
duck. Male has a vivid white
supercilium, and grey flanks
and upper forewings. Female
similar to female Teal, but with
stripier face pattern. Occurs on
lakes and freshwater marshes
in pairs or small parties, but
never in large flocks. Mainly
a summer visitor to Britain.

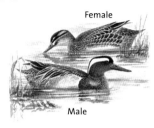

Female

Male

Scaup *Aythya marila*

Length 46cm. A diving duck.
Male similar to male Tufted
Duck, but with a grey back and
no crest on the head. Female
also similar to Tufted Duck,
but with white at the base of

Female

Male

the bill; upperparts and flanks greyish in winter, brownish in summer.
In Britain locally common on coasts in winter; rarely breeds.

Red-crested Pochard *Netta rufina*

Length 55cm. Large diving duck with a round head. Breeding male has
a bright orange head, black breast and neck, coral red bill and white
flanks. Non-breeding male is brown with a red bill. Female is brownish
with pale cheeks and a grey bill. Favours
well-vegetated wetlands. Scarce
resident in Britain with
growing feral population
in southern England.

Male

Female

Tufted Duck
Aythya fuligula

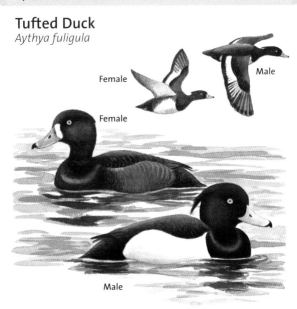

Female

Male

Female

Male

SIZE AND DESCRIPTION 43cm. A jaunty little diving duck. Drake is black and white with a drooping crest on the back of the head; duck is dark brown with the suggestion of a crest. Bill is blue with a dark tip.

VOICE Tends to be silent.

HABITAT Medium-sized or large fresh waters with fringing vegetation. More widespread in winter, when it occurs on more open gravel pits and reservoirs without cover. Widespread in Europe, wintering south to Mediterranean.

FOOD AND HABITS Dives deeper than Pochard, eating mostly insects and molluscs. Nests on the ground a few metres from the water's edge.

Pochard
Aythya ferina

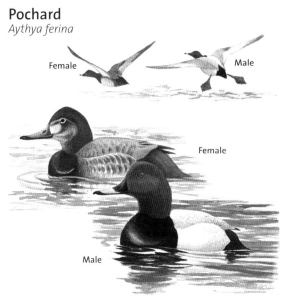

Female

Male

Female

Male

Female

Male

SIZE AND DESCRIPTION 46cm. Drake has a chestnut head, black breast, and grey back and flanks. Light-blue bill. Female is brown with a pale throat.

VOICE A quiet bird; male gives a soft whistle, female growls.

HABITAT Large ponds, lakes and slow-flowing streams with fringing vegetation. Outside breeding season can be seen on a wide range of freshwater bodies. Summer migrant in northern and eastern Europe, wintering in south and west.

FOOD AND HABITS A diving duck more active at night than during the day, and often seen resting on the water by day. Nest a down-lined grass cup well hidden on the ground.

Common Eider
Somateria mollissima

Young male

Female

Male

SIZE AND DESCRIPTION 60cm. The male of this large sea duck is
unmistakable in breeding plumage. Heads of both sexes have a
characteristic wedge shape with a long triangular bill. Non-breeding
male may appear almost black, or chequered black and white. Female
has brown-barred plumage.

VOICE Male makes a surprised-sounding 'ah-hoo', female stuttering
'kokokok' calls.

HABITAT Sea and rocky coastal areas. Much more common in north and
Scotland and Ireland, where it breeds, than in southern Britain. Very
rare inland.

FOOD AND HABITS Dives for crustaceans and molluscs. Nests on coastal
islands in colonies of 100–15,000 individuals.

Goldeneye
Bucephala clangula

Female

Male

Female

Male

Size and description 46cm. A diving duck. Conspicuous male is bright white and black with a glossy dark green head that has a circular white patch below the eye. Female and juvenile are grey with a brown head. In flight, makes a whistling noise with the wings.

Voice Rarely vocal. Male sometimes makes a disyllabic nasal call, female a harsh growl.

Habitat Found almost equally on coastal and inland waters. Mainly a winter visitor to Britain, also breeding occasionally in Scotland.

Food and habits Diet consists mainly of aquatic invertebrates, as well as amphibians, small fish and some plant material (mainly in autumn). Nests in hollows of mature trees.

Common Scoter
Melanitta nigra

Female

Male

SIZE AND DESCRIPTION 48cm. A sea duck. Male is black with a patch of bright yellow on the beak. Female is dark brown with pale cheeks.
VOICE A whistling 'pheeuu' in flight and while displaying.
HABITAT Most likely to be seen on the sea, and sometimes on large inland reservoirs. Breeds in north-east Europe, and winters in North Sea, Baltic and Atlantic. In Britain occasionally breeds on remote lochs in Scotland and Ireland; otherwise found mainly off coasts in winter.
FOOD AND HABITS Diet consists mostly of molluscs, and insects and fish eggs in freshwater habitats. Dives to 30m to hunt for shellfish. Congregates in large bobbing rafts of hundreds or thousands of birds well offshore.

Long-tailed Duck *Clangula hyemalis*

Length 58cm. A sea duck. Adult male has a very long tail. Plumage complex, with dark brown-and-white pattern of male almost reversed from non-breeding to breeding bird. Female and juvenile duller, brownish above and white below, with white blotches on the face. Breeds in north European tundra. Winters at sea south to Britain, where it is mainly coastal and more common in north than south.

Breeding male

Non-breeding male

Female

Velvet Scoter *Melanitta fusca*

Length 55cm. A sea duck often found with Common Scoters. Male similar in size and shape to Common Scoter, but has yellow on sides of beak, a white patch below the eye and a white speculum on the wings that may be visible when swimming. Female and juvenile have sooty plumage with pale patches on the head. Breeds in Scandinavia. Winters near coasts in Baltic, North Sea and Atlantic. In Britain occurs mainly along coasts.

Female

Male

Goosander
Mergus merganser

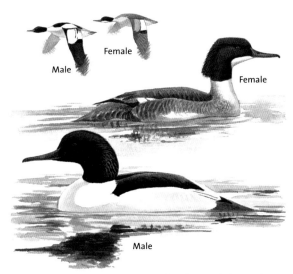

Male

Female

Female

Male

SIZE AND DESCRIPTION 62cm. Largest sawbill. Male is vivid white with a dark green head that looks black from a distance, and a slender hooked bright red bill. Female and juvenile are grey with a white breast and a brown head that has a slightly shaggy crest.

VOICE A quacking 'orr' during display.

HABITAT Lakes, rivers and shores. In Britain resident in north and winter visitor in south.

FOOD AND HABITS Diet consists mainly of fish, which it may pursue by swimming short distances. Nest down-lined in burrow or hollow tree.

Red-breasted Merganser
Mergus serrator

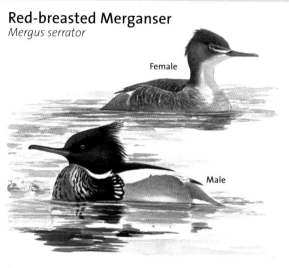

Female

Male

SIZE AND DESCRIPTION 55cm. Striking sawbill similar to Goosander, but less common. Male black above with flanks finely marked with grey, a white belly and a chestnut breast specked with dark brown. Head and crest are dark green, the throat white and the nape black. Female and juvenile are grey above, with a white belly and chestnut breast, nape and spiky crest.

VOICE Generally silent.

HABITAT Breeds beside rivers and lakes, and along sheltered coasts in northern Europe. Winters south to Black Sea. In Britain breeds in north and found around coasts in winter.

FOOD AND HABITS Feeds mainly on small fish; also small amounts of plant material and aquatic invertebrates. Nest down-lined in hollow or burrow.

Smew *Mergellus albellus*

Length 42cm. A small sawbill that has a relatively short bill. Male white with black stripes and a black eye-patch, and grey flanks. Female and juvenile grey with a red-brown cap, and white cheeks and throat. Breeds in tree hollows near lakes in taiga. Winters on rivers, lakes and sea south to England and Black Sea.

Female/juvenile

Male

Ruddy Duck *Oxyura jamaicensis*

Length 40cm. North American diving duck introduced to Britain. Small and dumpy with a raised stiff tail. Breeding male has a red-brown body, white cheeks and a blue bill that fades in winter. Female and juvenile are greyish-brown with a paler face and cheek-stripe. Male's courtship display includes producing a drumming sound by slapping the bill against the chest, and 'bobbing' and creating bubbles in front of it.

Female/ juvenile

Male

Ptarmigan *Lagopus muta*

Length 34cm. In winter all white except for black tail-tip and black lores (region between eye and bill on side of head) in male. In summer the head and upperparts are mottled grey and brown. A high-altitude species found year-round in northern tundra and high-altitude areas of Europe. In Britain occurs only on high mountains in Scotland.

Winter male

Summer female

Red Grouse *Lagopus lagopus*

Length 38cm. Adult male is mottled rich reddish-chestnut all over with red fleshy wattles over the eyes. Female is similar but with no wattles. In Britain found only on open treeless heather moorland in northern and western areas.

Male

Female

Capercaille *Tetrao urogallus*

Length, male 85cm; female 60cm. A large game bird. Male dark with a metallic blue-green sheen on the head and underparts, and brown wings. Smaller female cryptically marked grey-brown with rusty orange breast. Male renowned for spring display, which involves fanning out the tail and issuing a crescendo of rattling sounds, followed by a 'plop' and hissing. Occurs in old coniferous forests in mountains. In Britain occurs only in old pine forests in the Scottish Highlands.

Male

Female

Black Grouse *Tetrao tetrix*

Length, male 52cm; female 42cm. Male black with a distinctive lyre-shaped tail, and white undertail coverts and wingbar. Female similar to female Red Grouse. Males gather at leks in spring, where they display and utter clucking and hissing sounds. In Britain occurs on moors, heaths and mountains at edge of tree line, in northern England, Scotland and north Wales, where it is now very rare.

Lek

'Grey hen'

'Black cock'

Common Pheasant
Phasianus colchicus

Female

Male

SIZE AND DESCRIPTION Male 75–90cm; female 53–64cm. Male has a long, barred golden tail, a green head and red wattles. Some have a white ring around the neck. Female has a shorter tail and is buffish-brown.

VOICE A loud and hoarse metallic call, 'koo-krock', then usually whirring wingbeat.

HABITAT Woodlands, farmland with hedges, big gardens and reed beds in much of Europe.

FOOD AND HABITS Feeds on seeds, fruits, nuts and roots. Nest a grassy cup on the ground.

SIMILAR SPECIES Several species of exotic pheasant have been introduced to Britain. **Golden Pheasant** (*Chrysolophus pictus*) from China is scarce in England and Northern Ireland. Even rarer **Lady Amherst's Pheasant** (*C. amherstiae*) from China is found only in England.

Red-legged Partridge
Alectoris rufa

SIZE AND DESCRIPTION 34cm. An introduced species that is a little larger than the native Grey Partridge. White cheeks and throat, flanks barred with white, black and chestnut, and a red bill and legs separate it from Grey Partridge.

VOICE Harsh 'chucka, chucka'.

HABITAT Open country and farmland; found in rather drier areas than Grey Partridge.

FOOD AND HABITS Mainly eats seeds and plant matter. Nests on the ground among grass or tall vegetation, or under a bush.

Grey Partridge
Perdix perdix

Male

Juvenile

Female

SIZE AND DESCRIPTION 30cm. A grey-brown bird. Male has a horseshoe-shaped chestnut patch on the breast. Whirring flight.

VOICE Loud 'kar-wit, kar-wit'; rapid cackling when startled into flight.

HABITAT Farmland, open country, moorland and heath across much of Europe, but becoming increasingly rare.

FOOD AND HABITS Eats mainly seeds, cereals and flower buds; insects an important food for chicks. Substantial population decline due to use of herbicides.

▶ **SIMILAR SPECIES Quail** (*Coturnix coturnix*). At 18cm long Britain's smallest game bird, and the only migrant one. Plumage basically pale yellow-brown. Conceals itself in dense vegetation in meadows and fields; usually only identifiable from call, 'whip whip-whip'. Scarce summer visitor to Britain.

Female

Male

Red-throated Diver
Gavia stellata

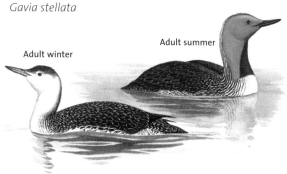

Adult summer

Adult winter

Size and description 60cm. Distinctive breeding plumage includes a brick-red throat, and a grey head and neck. At other times mainly grey-brown above, with white on the face that extends to above the eye. Slender upturned bill; swims with head mostly tilted upwards.

Voice Song an eerie wailing, heard in breeding areas. Flight call a goose-like 'ak ak'.

Habitat Breeds on lakes in northern Europe, including Scotland, and winters on coasts and large inland lakes.

Food and habits Primarily a fish-eater; may also feed on molluscs, crustaceans, frogs and plant material. Spears prey underwater, diving to 2–9m in depth. Nest is always close to water.

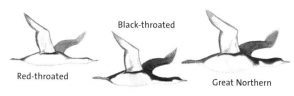

Red-throated

Black-throated

Great Northern

Black-throated Diver *Gavia arctica*

Length 70cm. Elegant diver that swims with its head and straight bill kept horizontal. Plumage of breeding bird includes a black chin and throat, and a grey hind-neck. Non-breeding bird basically black above and white below. Song an eerie wailing uttered in breeding season. In Europe breeds on northern lakes; winters at sea, and sometimes on lakes and reservoirs. In Britain breeds rarely on Scottish lochs.

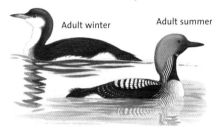

Adult winter

Adult summer

Great Northern Diver *Gavia immer*

Length 80cm. Similar to Black-throated Diver, but with a stouter bill and steeper forehead. Breeding plumage is black with white neck-bands and chequering on the mantle. In Europe breeds in Iceland; winters in North Sea and north Atlantic. In Britain found on sea and coastal estuaries, and rarely on inland waters.

Adult winter

Adult summer

Great Crested Grebe
Podiceps cristatus

SIZE AND DESCRIPTION 48cm. Unmistakable in breeding plumage; both sexes have a large horned crest and ruff, which are lost in winter. Chicks are striped.

VOICE Generally silent. Call usually a harsh bark; crooning song.

HABITAT Breeds on still waters, lakes, ponds and reservoirs, and slow-flowing rivers. May be found on coasts and estuaries in winter. Occurs in much of Europe except far north.

FOOD AND HABITS Dives for food, which consists mostly of fish and invertebrates, and some plant matter. Often ingests feathers. Nests on a floating mat of reeds and other water plants near the water's edge.

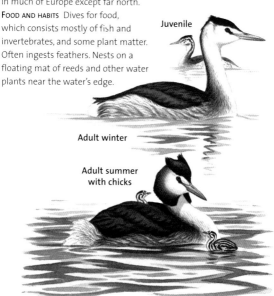

Juvenile

Adult winter

Adult summer
with chicks

Slavonian Grebe *Podiceps auritus*

Length 35cm. Breeding bird has a splendid black head, erect yellow ear tufts and a red neck. On the Continent breeds on reed-fringed ponds in north-east; winters in north-west and south-east. Uncommon in Britain, breeding only on a few Scottish lochs.

Adult winter

Adult summer

Black-necked Grebe *Podiceps nigricollis*

Length 32 cm. Breeding bird has distinctive yellow ear-tufts and a black head. Non-breeding plumage similar to Slavonian's. Breeds further south, in colonies on shallow lakes. Winters on lakes and coasts south to Mediterranean. Uncommon in Britain; rarely breeds.

Adult summer

Adult winter

Red-necked Grebe *Podiceps grisegena*

Length 45cm. Similar to but considerably smaller than Great-crested Grebe. Red neck and no head ornament in breeding plumage. On the Continent breeds on reed-fringed lakes in north-east. Winters on coasts of North and Black Seas, and Adriatic. Uncommon in Britain.

Adult summer

Adult winter

Little Grebe
Tachybaptus ruficollis

Juvenile

Adult winter

Adult summer

SIZE AND DESCRIPTION 27cm. The Little Grebe, or Dabchick, in breeding plumage has bright chestnut cheeks and throat, and dark brown upperparts. In winter it is grey, but still has the abrupt 'powder-puff' rear. Sexes are similar.

VOICE Whinnying song.

HABITAT Still and slow-moving waters from ponds to rivers in much of Europe except far north.

FOOD AND HABITS Dives for food, mostly small fish. Rather skulking. Nests among waterside vegetation such as rushes, or under overhanging branches.

Fulmar
Fulmarus glacialis

Adults

SIZE AND DESCRIPTION 47cm. Seabird that resembles a gull, usually having grey upperparts and white underparts, but with a rather thick neck. Wings are held straight and stiff in flight. Nostrils are located in short tubes halfway down the bill.

VOICE Guttural chuckles and growls mainly at nest.

HABITAT Coasts, cliffs and sea.

FOOD AND HABITS Eats fish, offal and molluscs. Nests in colonies on cliff faces. Returns to breeding sites from November onwards, dispersing in late summer. Flight interspersed with frequent glides.

Manx Shearwater *Puffinus puffinus*

Sooty Shearwater *Puffinus griseus*

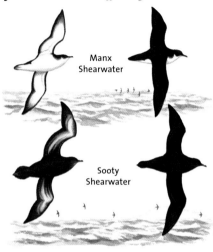

Manx Shearwater

Sooty Shearwater

SIZE AND DESCRIPTION Manx 32cm; Sooty 45cm. Manx is black above, white below, with a stiff-winged flight. It glides low over the waves, well out at sea. Sooty is larger and much darker, and has silvery underwings.

VOICE Howling calls when visiting colony at night.

HABITAT Manx: coastal islands mainly off Britain. Nests in burrows in the ground, but otherwise pelagic. Sooty: breeds in island burrows in southern hemisphere, passing through north Atlantic in late summer. Rare in Britain, occuring most often off south-west headlands.

FOOD AND HABITS Food mainly small fish, squid and crustaceans.

European Storm-petrel *Hydrobates pelagicus*

Leach's Storm-petrel *Oceanodroma leucorhoa*

European Storm-petrel

Leach's Storm-petrel

SIZE AND DESCRIPTION European 15cm; Leach's 21cm. European is tiny, resembling a House Martin from above. Smaller and darker than Leach's, with rounder wings, a white bar on the underwing and a square tail. Leach's has longer and more pointed wings and a slightly forked tail. More buoyant, tern-like flight than European, which flaps without gliding.

VOICE Purring and grunting at night-time at nest sites.

HABITAT Nest in burrows on islands, but otherwise pelagic.

FOOD AND HABITS Feed mainly on surface plankton and small fish, which are taken from the water's surface without alighting.

Gannet
Morus bassanas

SIZE AND DESCRIPTION 90cm. Large seabird with long narrow wings that have black tips, a pointed tail, a long and pointed blue-white bill, and a yellow tinge to the back of the neck. Juveniles are dark, becoming lighter as they mature at three years of age.

VOICE Harsh croaks at nest.

HABITAT Entirely maritime, only coming to land to breed. In Britain breeds on northern and western coasts in Scotland and Wales. Can be seen offshore almost anywhere, especially when migrating south in autumn.

FOOD AND HABITS Diet almost exclusively fish, which are caught by spectacular arrow-shaped plunge-dives from heights of 15–30m. Nests in dense colonies on cliffs and rocky islands.

Cormorant
Phalacrocorax carbo

Breeding

Adult non-breeding

Juvenile

Breeding

SIZE AND DESCRIPTION 90cm. Very dark seabird with a white throat and cheek patches, black-bronze upperparts and blue-black underparts. White thigh patch in breeding season, when some birds also have a white head. Swims low in the water. On land 'heraldic' pose with wings held out is characteristic. Sexes are similar; juvenile is brown.

VOICE At nest makes guttural noises.

HABITAT Present throughout the year on coast; sometimes inland on islands on lakes and rivers.

FOOD AND HABITS Eats fish almost exclusively, catching them by diving. Nests in colonies, usually on rocks on coast.

Shag
Phalacrocorax aristotelis

Non-breeding

Juvenile

Breeding

SIZE AND DESCRIPTION 75cm. Similar to Cormorant except in full breeding plumage, when Shag has a greener sheen and a quiff on its head. There is also a thick yellow gape reaching beyond the eye, there are no white patches and the forehead is steeper than that of a Cormorant.
VOICE Harsh croaks on breeding ground.
HABITAT Year-round resident of rocky coasts and nearby seas. Very unusual inland, unlike Cormorant. Local along coasts of Europe, north-west Russia and North Africa.
FOOD AND HABITS Feeds on fish, which are taken mostly by diving from the surface. Semi-colonial or solitary breeding bird.

Grey Heron
Ardea cinerea

Breeding

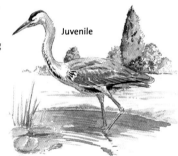

Juvenile

SIZE AND DESCRIPTION 95cm. Very large and mainly grey, with black-and-white markings. Breeding plumage includes long black plumes on head. Neck is tucked back in flight; wingbeats are slow and ponderous.

VOICE Flight call a hoarse croaking 'kraark' and 'chraa'; bill-clapping at nest.

HABITAT Year round in marshes, ponds, lakes, rivers, canals, flooded fields and estuaries throughout Europe.

FOOD AND HABITS Feeds on fish, amphibians, small mammals, insects and reptiles. Hunts by stalking slowly through shallow water, or standing motionless waiting for prey to come within reach, when it strikes with lightning speed. Nests in colonies, usually high in tall trees, in a huge nest.

Little Egret
Egretta garzetta

Size and description 60cm. A very graceful white heron. Black bill and black legs with yellow toes. Long white plumes on nape and back in breeding plumage.

Voice Flight call is a harsh 'ktchar'.

Habitat Estuaries, marshes, rivers, saline lagoons and other shallow water bodies. Local in southern and central Europe. Increasingly common in Britain and Ireland since the 1990s, and now a common resident along coast in much of England and Wales.

Food and habits Diet consists of various animals such as small fish, amphibians and insects. Nests colonially in bushes near wetlands.

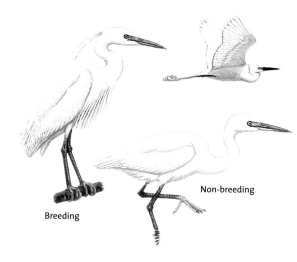

Non-breeding

Breeding

Bittern
Botaurus stellaris

Adults

SIZE AND DESCRIPTION 75cm. Plumage brown marbled and striped with buff and black, offering good camouflage against dead reeds in its habitat. Freezes in an upright position when alarmed.

VOICE In spring male utters a far-carrying booming 'woomb' or 'oo-hoo-oomb', like a foghorn, mainly at night. Call in flight a barking 'cow'.

HABITAT Large freshwater reed beds year-round in much of central Europe. Rarely breeds in Britain, and more widespread in winter.

FOOD AND HABITS Diet consists of fish, frogs, insects, small mammals and birds, and snakes. Hunts by walking slowly among plants, lifting its feet high with each step. Nest a reed platform among reeds. Declined alarmingly in the 1990s, but recent successful conservation measures have resulted in an encouraging increase in the population.

Spoonbill
Platalea leucorodia

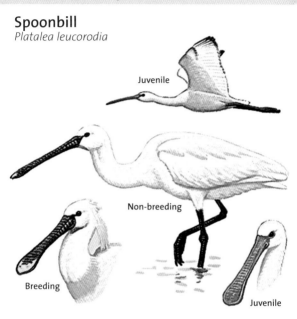

Juvenile

Non-breeding

Breeding

Juvenile

SIZE AND DESCRIPTION 85cm. Unmistakable large white bird with a long flat bill that broadens at the tip.

HABITAT On the Continent breeds in large reed beds around shallow wetlands in south and the Netherlands. Winters in western Europe and Africa. In Britain most likely at one of east coast nature reserves in spring or autumn; in winter a few mainly on southern estuaries.

FOOD AND HABITS Feeds on molluscs by sieving water with side-to-side head movement. Nests colonially in platform nests erected in large reed beds. Rare in Britain and of European conservation concern.

Red Kite
Milvus milvus

Adult

Adult

SIZE AND DESCRIPTION 61cm. Grey head, body russet above and below, white patch on underwing and deeply forked tail, which is twisted and turned in flight.

VOICE Mewing call, higher-pitched than Common Buzzard's.

HABITAT Deciduous woodland and open countryside. British population (Wales only) augmented by recent successful reintroductions in England, Scotland and Ireland.

FOOD AND HABITS Feeds chiefly on earthworms, and also mammals (especially rabbits), birds and carrion. Nests in trees.

Hen Harrier
Circus cyaneus

Male

Male

Female

Female

Female

SIZE AND DESCRIPTION 45cm. Slimmer build and narrower wings than Marsh Harrier. Male grey with white underparts.

VOICE Display call 'tchik-ikikikik'.

HABITAT Moorland, farmland and marshes. Scarce in Britain. Breeds in small numbers on treeless moorlands; more widespread in winter, frequently on coast.

FOOD AND HABITS Diet includes small mammals, birds, reptiles, insects and carrion. Nest a grassy platform on the ground.

▼ **SIMILAR SPECIES Montagu's Harrier** (*C. pygargus*). Slighter and rarer than Hen Harrier, with more pointed wings. Underparts speckled with brown. Voice higher than Hen Harrier's. Summer visitor breeding in a few sites mainly in eastern England.

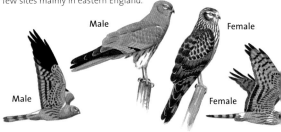

Male

Male

Female

Male

Female

Marsh Harrier
Circus aeruginosus

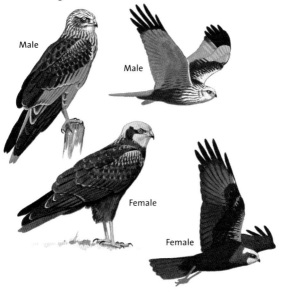

Male

Male

Female

Female

Size and description 52cm. Largest European harrier. Usually dark brown above with buff shoulders and head. Male has a grey tail and grey secondaries. Often flies with wings held in a shallow 'V'.

Voice Two-note display call, 'kweeoo'.

Habitat Reed beds and marshes. Summer visitor to central and eastern Europe, including Britain; resident year-round in south.

Food and habits Eats small mammals, frogs, and birds and their eggs. Hunts by systematically quartering the ground. Nests in reed beds.

Common Buzzard
Buteo buteo

SIZE AND DESCRIPTION 52cm. Large with broad rounded wings and a short tail. Usually dark brown above with variable amounts of white below; sometimes with a dark carpal patch.

VOICE Mewing cry, 'peeioo'.

HABITAT Moorland and agricultural land. Year-round resident across much of Europe; summer visitor to far north.

Dark form

FOOD AND HABITS Feeds mainly on small mammals, which it catches with a low-flying pounce; also carrion. Soars on V-shaped wings. Nest is a bulky structure of twigs, usually erected in a tree.

SIMILAR SPECIES **Rough-legged Buzzard** (*B. lagopus*), 54cm long, has a white tail with a broad black band near the tip. Breeds in mountains in northern Europe, wintering in open areas south to Britain (mainly east coast) and Black Sea. **Honey Buzzard** (*Pernis apivorus*), 54cm long, has a smaller head than the Common Buzzard, and soars on flat wings. Feeds mainly on wasps, digging out their nests. Summer visitor to much of Europe; scarce in Britain. Winters in Africa.

Pale form

Sparrowhawk
Accipiter nisus

SIZE AND DESCRIPTION 35cm. Wings blunt and broad. Male much smaller than female, and has a blue-grey head and back, and breast barred with rusty-red. Female has grey-brown barring on the breast and a pale 'eyebrow'.

VOICE Monotonous ringing call near nest.

HABITAT Woodland, parks, gardens and hedgerows. Breeds across Europe. British populations are mainly resident.

FOOD AND HABITS Small birds are the main food of Sparrowhawks, which hunt by ambushing their prey. Nest a platform of twigs high up in tree canopy.

Northern Goshawk
Accipiter gentilis

Juvenile

Adult

SIZE AND DESCRIPTION 55cm. Similar to Sparrowhawk, but much larger and rarer. Male grey-brown above with white underparts barred with black. Juvenile brown above with buff underparts vertically streaked with darker brown.

VOICE Call 'kyow-kyow-kyow' and drawn-out 'peeeyee'.

HABITAT Lives deep in dense forests across much of Europe. Rare resident in Britain.

FOOD AND HABITS Diet consists mainly of small mammals and birds. Nest a platform of twigs high up in canopy.

Golden Eagle *Aquila chrysaetos*

Length 85 cm. Adult rich dark brown with a paler head and neck. Tail long and broad; bill massive and hooked. Wingspan more than 2m. Rarely vocal; call a rough 'kaah'. Inhabits remote European mountains and forests. In Britain mainly in southern and eastern Scotland. Diet includes rodents, rabbits, carrion, reptiles, birds, fish and large insects. Territory may be 155sq km for pair. Nest a massive branch structure on a high rocky ledge or in a tree. Widespread but never numerous.

Adult

Adult

White-tailed Eagle *Haliaetus albicilla*

Length 85 cm. Adult massive. Mainly brown with paler head and neck, yellow bill and distinctive white tail. Broad 'barn door' wings. Tail and bill darker in juvenile. Inhabits old forests near large wetlands in Europe. In Britain reintroduced to Scotland and Ireland; a rare breeder. Diet includes fish, birds and carrion. Nest huge, of sticks in a tree or on a coastal cliff.

Adult

Adult

Osprey
Pandion haliaetus

SIZE AND DESCRIPTION 55cm.
Large and graceful fish-eating
bird of prey that has dark
brown upperparts and white
underparts. Long narrow wings
are held angled in flight.

VOICE Call a short shrill whistle.

HABITAT Lakes, lochs and rivers; reservoirs on
passage. Uncommon in Britain; breeds in Scotland, and in smaller
numbers in Wales and northern England. May be seen at almost any
large body of fresh water during spring and autumn migration.

FOOD AND HABITS Feeds on fish, which it catches by plunge-diving from
10–30m. Flies holding fish in talons in line with its own head and tail.
Nests in tall trees.

Kestrel
Falco tinnunculus

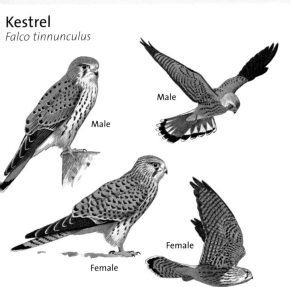

Male

Male

Male

Female

Female

Female

SIZE AND DESCRIPTION 34cm. Distinctive long tail and pointed wings. Male has a grey head, black-tipped grey tail and dark-flecked russet back. Female and juvenile lack the grey head, and have a brown tail with narrow bars, and more dark flecks on the back.

VOICE Noisy at nest-site; rasping 'kee-kee-kee-kee' call.

HABITAT Farmland, moorland and other open areas. Breeds in cities and towns; may be seen flying over gardens. Resident across Europe; northern and eastern European populations migrate during autumn.

FOOD AND HABITS Hovers above grassland or perches on trees and pylons, ready to drop down on rodents in grass. Also feeds on small birds, large insects and lizards. Lays eggs in a hole or on a bare ledge.

Merlin
Falco columbarius

Male

Female

SIZE AND DESCRIPTION 29cm. Small and compact falcon with short
pointed wings. Male blue-grey above and buff with dark spots below,
with indistinct moustaches. Female and juvenile brown above.

VOICE Calls are 'kee-kee-kee'.

HABITAT British breeding population is at the south-west limit of the
species' European range; thinly scattered across upland moorland
from south-west England north to Shetland. Often found on coast in
winter. Nowhere common.

FOOD AND HABITS Feeds on small birds, which it hunts in fast flight close
to the ground. Nest usually on the ground, among heather.

Peregrine Falcon
Falco peregrinus

Adult

Juvenile

Adult

Juvenile

Size and description 45cm. Large and
compact falcon with a heavy build.
Adults have strong black moustaches
and horizontal barring on underparts,
and are bluish steely-grey above. Female
larger than male. Largest British falcon.
Voice Calls are 'kee-kee-kee'.
Habitat Cliffs, mountains, towns and open areas throughout Europe.
Breeds on cliffs, rock faces and high buildings.
Food and habits Feeds on birds, including feral pigeons. Circles high up
waiting for prey to fly below, then plunges at high speed in pursuit.
Eggs laid in a bare scrape.

Hobby
Falco subbuteo

Juvenile

Adult

SIZE AND DESCRIPTION 32cm. Dashing little falcon that looks like a large swift in flight. Dark slaty-grey above with dark moustaches on white cheeks and throat, and red thighs.

VOICE A repeated clear 'kew-kew-kew'.

HABITAT Mostly heathlands, where it often nests in pine trees. Summer visitor to Britain.

FOOD AND HABITS Feeds on small birds, and large insects such as dragonflies, which are often eaten in flight. Usually nests in an abandoned crow's nest.

Water Rail
Rallus aquaticus

Juvenile

Adult

SIZE AND DESCRIPTION 24cm. A secretive bird that is often hidden in reeds and more often heard than seen. Grey underparts, white-barred flanks, a red bill and a pointed tail that is usually held erect.

VOICE Pig-like squeaking and grunting, and a high-pitched 'kip-kip'. Male display call 'kurp kurp kurp', female 'tchik-tchik'.

HABITAT Reed beds and other densely vegetated wetland. Widespread in Europe; summer visitor in north.

FOOD AND HABITS Omnivorous. Diet consists mainly of small animals such as worms, molluscs, shrimps, crayfish, spiders, insects, amphibians and fish; also feeds on plant matter. Nest a cup of vegetation, usually on a thick stand of reeds or rushes.

Spotted Crake
Porzana porzana

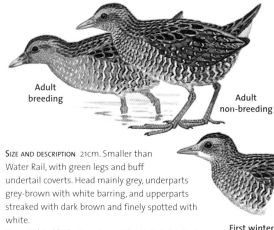

**Adult
breeding**

**Adult
non-breeding**

First winter

SIZE AND DESCRIPTION 21cm. Smaller than
Water Rail, with green legs and buff
undertail coverts. Head mainly grey, underparts
grey-brown with white barring, and upperparts
streaked with dark brown and finely spotted with
white.

VOICE Whip-like 'quip, quip, quip' call at night during
breeding season.

HABITAT Occurs on marshes and flooded meadows throughout
Europe except far north. Winters in Africa and India. Rare and difficult
to see in Britain.

FOOD AND HABITS Probes mud and shallow water with bill to pick up
invertebrates; also hunts by sight. Nests in marsh vegetation.

Corncrake
Crex crex

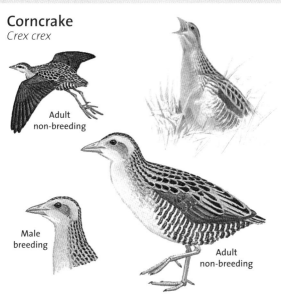

Adult
non-breeding

Male
breeding

Adult
non-breeding

SIZE AND DESCRIPTION 23cm. Another rail that is rarely seen. Breast greyish, flanks barred rufous and rusty-brown wing coverts.

VOICE Display call a repeated relentless wooden rasping, 'rrrp-rrrp', often uttered at night.

HABITAT In Europe occurs on wet meadows with tall grass and grain fields. Winters in Africa. Declining in Britain and very rare outside Western Isles.

FOOD AND HABITS Diet includes insects, spiders and other invertebrates. Builds nest from dead stems and leaves in dense vegetation. Declining everywhere due to modern farming practices such as mechanical mowing of fields, in which it nests.

Moorhen
Gallinula chloropus

SIZE AND DESCRIPTION 30CM. Distinctive slaty plumage, dark brown wings, white undertail coverts, yellow-tipped red bill and green legs. Flicks tail as it walks with a careful tread. Juvenile is brown.
VOICE Varied repertoire includes harsh metallic 'krrek' and 'kittick' calls.
HABITAT Ponds, rivers, canals, lakes and marshes across Europe. Also parks and gardens with large ponds.
FOOD AND HABITS Feeds on seeds, insects, molluscs, leaves and carrion. Nest a bulky mound of vegetation on the water. Juveniles may help parents raise next generation.

Juvenile

Adult

Coot
Fulica atra

SIZE AND DESCRIPTION 38cm. Mainly black water bird with a white bill and shield on the forehead, greenish legs and a domed back. Chicks are black with rufous heads. Juvenile is greyish.

VOICE Quite noisy; call usually a loud 'kowk' or variation.

HABITAT Still and slow-moving fresh water. Usually found on larger and more open water bodies than Moorhen.

FOOD AND HABITS Dives for food, largely aquatic plants. Often in flocks, especially outside the breeding season. Requires fringing vegetation for nesting. Quarrelsome; fights on the water using its large feet, especially during the breeding season, when it will attack birds much larger than itself such as swans and geese.

Juvenile

Adult

Oystercatcher
Haematopus ostralegus

Summer

Winter

Size and description 43cm. A large and boldly marked black-and-white wader with an orange-red bill and pink legs. White rump and wing bar, and white collar in winter.

Voice Noisy; loud 'kleep' call and piping display.

Habitat Coasts, mudflats and wet meadows; usually coastal. Resident in Britain; also passage migrant and winter visitor.

Food and habits Eats mainly invertebrates, especially molluscs, which it opens by hammering or prising (some Oystercatchers have pointed bills, others have squarer-ended bills). Nests on the ground.

Avocet
Recurvirostra avosetta

SIZE AND DESCRIPTION 43cm. Large, elegant and boldly marked black-and-white wader with a black crown and nape, blue-grey legs and a slender upturned bill.

VOICE Call a liquid 'kluut'.

HABITAT Salt marshes, brackish lagoons and mudflats. Mainly summer visitor to Britain, breeding mostly in East Anglia and south-east England. Winters in south-west and west Africa, but many birds stay in western Europe in mild winters.

FOOD AND HABITS Feeds chiefly on shrimp-like crustaceans, ragworms, other invertebrates and fish spawn, using vigorous sideways swishes of bill through water and silty mud. Nest lined with marsh vegetation in a shallow scrape on the ground.

Juvenile

Adult

Stone-curlew
Burhinus oedicnemus

SIZE AND DESCRIPTION 42cm. Unmistakable bird with cryptic brown plumage, a large yellow eye, long yellow legs and a yellow bill tipped with black. Colour of plumage ensures that it is well camouflaged against stony ground, especially when it freezes.

VOICE Call a whistling 'crew-li' or 'tree-iel' like that of a Curlew.

HABITAT Steppes and heaths. In Europe resident only in Spain, and a summer visitor elsewhere. Breeds locally on sandy heaths and adjacent farmland in southern England (East Anglia, Dorset and Hampshire).

FOOD AND HABITS Feeds on insects, molluscs, small lizards, seeds and sometimes small mammals. Eggs laid in a bare scrape on the ground.

Adult

Dotterel *Charadrius morinellus*

Length 22cm. Distinctive
plover with an orange
lower breast and flanks,
white breast-band and
vivid white eyebrow.
Female brighter
than male, and
juvenile paler than
adult. Breeds on
European tundra
and mountain
meadows. Winters in Spain
and north Africa. In Britain breeds
only on mountain-tops in Scottish
Highlands; seen rarely on passage in
'trips' or small flocks elsewhere.

Juvenile

Female
summer

Kentish Plover *Charadrius alexandrinus*

Length 16cm. Pale dainty plover with
a large head, black legs and patches on
the sides of its breast. Breeding male
has a rufous crown and small black
patches on its breast. Like juvenile
Ringed Plover. Occurs on sandy beaches
and tidal meadows, as well as locally
on inland salt lakes. Summer visitor
to northern Europe, wintering in
Mediterranean. Rare visitor to Britain.

Male
summer

Ringed Plover
Charadrius hiaticula

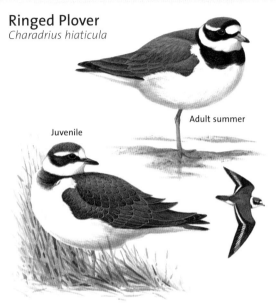

Adult summer

Juvenile

SIZE AND DESCRIPTION 19cm. Common shore bird with a black mask and breast band, and a white collar and forehead. Upperparts brown, underparts white. Narrow white wingbar. Black markings more subdued in winter than in summer.

VOICE Calls a liquid 'tooi' and 'kluup'. Trilling song.

HABITAT Breeds on beaches and mudflats; also lake edges or tundra, sometimes inland, in north. Winters mainly on rocky and muddy coasts in western Europe.

FOOD AND HABITS Mainly eats insects, worms and molluscs, and some plant matter. Nests in a shallow scrape on the ground.

Little Ringed Plover
Charadrius dubius

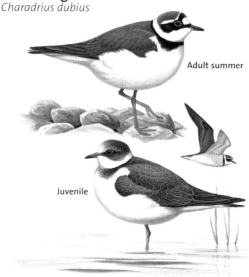

Adult summer

Juvenile

SIZE AND DESCRIPTION 16cm. Very similar to Ringed Plover, but less common, and adults have a golden eyering, duller straw-coloured legs and a black bill. No narrow white wingbar.

VOICE Calls a whistling 'tiu'. Display or flight call a rough rolling 'chrechrechrechre'.

HABITAT Inland marshes, lakes and gravel pits. Summer visitor to most of Europe. In Britain fairly common in south, but absent from north.

FOOD AND HABITS Diet consists mainly of insects, as well as spiders, freshwater shrimps and other small crustaceans. Nest a shallow scrape on loose sand, dry mud or rocks, or in sparse vegetation, near water.

Golden Plover
Pluvialis apricaria

SIZE AND DESCRIPTION 28cm. Breeding plumage spangled yellow and brown, with black throat and belly, northern birds being more boldly marked. Outside breeding season black on underparts is absent.
VOICE Liquid whistling call, 'tlui'. Song a liquid 'too-roo, too-roo'.
HABITAT Breeds on moorland and tundra in northern Europe. Flocks in winter on farmland and meadows in southern and western Europe.
FOOD AND HABITS Eats mostly insects, molluscs and some plant matter. Nest a grass-lined scrape well hidden on the ground.

Adult winter

Adult summer

Grey Plover
Pluvialis squatarola

Adult summer

Adult winter

SIZE AND DESCRIPTION 28cm. A strikingly handsome plover. Adult in summer has silver-grey black-flecked upperparts, separated from the black face, throat, breast and belly by a wide margin. Winter adult and juvenile paler and duller. Bill and legs black.

VOICE Call a plaintive three-syllable 'plee-oo-ee'.

HABITAT Mudflats and estuaries along coasts of North Sea, Atlantic and Mediterranean. Breeds on northern tundra. In Britain common on coast and present all year except midsummer.

FOOD AND HABITS Feeds mostly on insects, and some plant matter in breeding season; on marine polychaete worms, molluscs and crustaceans in winter. Nest a shallow scrape on dry ground in an exposed stony site.

Lapwing
Vanellus vanellus

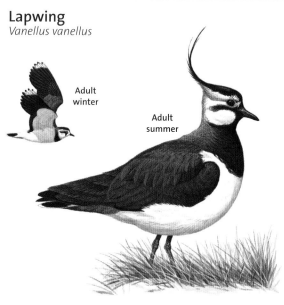

Adult winter

Adult summer

SIZE AND DESCRIPTION 30cm. Dark and glossy metallic-green upperparts, white below with a buff undertail, and a long wispy crest. Throat black in breeding season. Juvenile has a short crest. Floppy, loose, broad-winged flight. Tumbling display flight by males in spring.
VOICE Calls 'peewit'.
HABITAT Farmland, grassland, moorland and marshes; also coasts and estuaries in winter. Winters in southern and western Europe.
FOOD AND HABITS Diet includes insects, worms and molluscs, with some vegetable matter. Nests on the ground. Winter flocks may be mixed with Golden Plovers.

Dunlin
Calidris alpina

SIZE AND DESCRIPTION
19cm.Slightly smaller
than Sanderling, with
longer bill and less
conspicuous white
wingbar. Summer
plumage scaly black
and brown above, and
white below with a
large black belly patch.
In winter it is greyer
with a whitish belly.

VOICE Call in flight 'treep'.

HABITAT Summer visitor

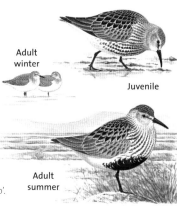

Adult
winter

Juvenile

Adult
summer

or resident breeding on northern tundra, upland moorland, marshes
and bogs. Outside breeding season occurs on seashores, mudflats,
creeks and estuaries on European coast; also visits inland waters.

FOOD AND HABITS Feeds on small invertebrates such as molluscs and
worms. Nest a grassy cup well hidden on the ground.

▶ SIMILAR SPECIES Pectoral Sandpiper
(*C. melanotos*). 19cm (female) and
22cm (male) long. Legs and base of
bill are pale; the densely streaked
breast is sharply demarcated from
the belly. Call a wooden 'drrrrk'.
Breeds on north-east Siberian and
North American tundra. Rare
migrant to marshes and mudflats
in Europe, including Britain.

Juvenile

Curlew Sandpiper
Calidris ferruginea

SIZE AND DESCRIPTION 20cm. Elegant sandpiper with a long curved bill, and a long neck and legs. Breeding plumage (rarely seen in Britain) includes a striking deep rufous colour on the breast and head. Juvenile has neatly scaled sandy brown upperparts and white flanks.
VOICE Call a disyllabic 'chirrip'.
HABITAT Breeds on Russian High Arctic tundra. Migrates via Europe to Africa. In Britain most likely to be seen on passage in spring or autumn.
FOOD AND HABITS Diet includes snails, worms and insects. Forages by probing mud rapidly with bill.

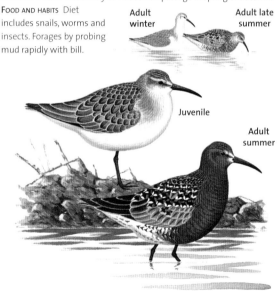

Adult winter

Adult late summer

Juvenile

Adult summer

Little Stint
Calidris minuta

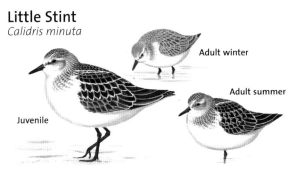

Adult winter

Adult summer

Juvenile

SIZE AND DESCRIPTION 15 cm. Tiny wader with black legs and a short, fine black beak. Winter plumage (rarely seen in Britain) soft grey with white underparts. Breeding plumage rufous on head and breast, turning buff-brown by July.

VOICE Call a feeble short 'pip'.

HABITAT Breeds on tundra in far north. On passage widespread on marshes and mudflats in coastal areas of Europe.

FOOD AND HABITS Feeds mainly on insects; also crustaceans and molluscs.

▼ **SIMILAR SPECIES** **Temminck's Stint** (*C. temminckii*). 14cm long, with a longer body than Little Stint, pale yellow legs and a soft trilling call. Breeds in north European wetlands. Rarer than Little, although a few breed in Scotland.

Adult winter

Adult summer

Juvenile

Knot
Calidris canutus

Adult summer

Juvenile

Adult winter

SIZE AND DESCRIPTION 25cm. A little larger than Dunlin, with a comparatively short bill. Winter plumage is grey. Narrow white wingbar. Breeding plumage is rufous.

VOICE Call 'knut'.

HABITAT Breeds on High Arctic tundra. Widespread on mudflats on North Sea and Atlantic coasts during migration and winter.

FOOD AND HABITS Feeds on invertebrates such as insects, molluscs, earthworms and crustaceans. Usually seen in flocks, which can be very large and dense. Spectacular aerial manoeuvres as flocks come in to roost. Nest a grass-lined scrape well hidden on the ground.

Sanderling
Calidris alba

Adult winter

Juvenile

Adult summer

SIZE AND DESCRIPTION 20cm. Pale grey in winter plumage. Summer plumage scaly brown above and on the breast; white belly shows white wingbar in all plumages.

VOICE In flight, liquid 'twick, twick'.

HABITAT Breeds further north than Britain, where it is a passage migrant and winter visitor confined to coast.

FOOD AND HABITS Distinctive feeding method as it runs in and out on the shore with the movement of the waves, often likened to a clockwork toy. Nest a grassy cup well hidden on the ground.

Purple Sandpiper *Calidris maritima*

21cm long. Dark grey plumage, uniform-looking in non-breeding bird and juvenile, scalier-looking in breeding bird, with rufous on the crown, ear-coverts, mantle and sides of the breast, and black-brown spots on the breast and flanks. Stout and decurved bill. Voice a soft 'kutt, ke-vutt'. Breeds on stony tundra. Winters south to Biscay along rocky coastlines and jetties. Gregarious in non-breeding season, forming small flocks.

Spotted Redshank *Tringa erythropus*

30cm long. Breeding birds almost black with a few white spots and a white eye-ring. Non-breeding birds soft grey above and white below. Plain upper wing with no wing bar, barred tail and white patch extending up back, and darker wings than Redshank's. Call also very different – a clear 'tchuit'. Passage migrant in Britain, mainly to southern areas. Large gatherings may occur in estuaries and coastal marshes.

Redshank
Tringa totanus

Adult winter

Juvenile

Adult summer

SIZE AND DESCRIPTION 28cm. Grey-brown wader with an orange-red bill and legs. Plumage greyer in winter than in summer. White rump and trailing edges to wings noticeable in flight.

VOICE Variety of yelping calls. Song, 'tu-udle...', may be given in flight or from the ground.

HABITAT Breeds on flood meadows, grassland and lowland moors both near coast and inland. Winters on coast, especially estuaries and mudflats. Most widespread on passage.

FOOD AND HABITS Feeds mostly on invertebrates. Often perches conspicuously on posts. Nest a deep cup hidden in a grass tussock.

Greenshank
Tringa nebularia

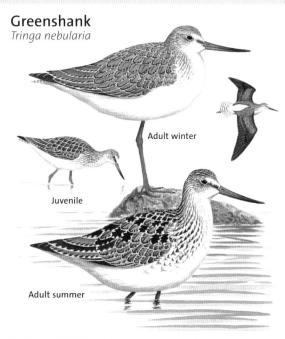

Adult winter

Juvenile

Adult summer

SIZE AND DESCRIPTION 32cm. A rather pale, grey wader. Legs are green. In flight shows a white tail, rump and lower back.

VOICE Lower pitched call than Redshank. Song, 'ru-tu, ru-tu ...', given in flight or while perched.

HABITAT Breeds in north European wetlands and open forests. Widespread on marshes and mudflats during migration.

FOOD AND HABITS Feeds almost entirely on invertebrates, amphibians and fish. Nests in a scrape well hidden on the ground.

Wood Sandpiper
Tringa glareola

SIZE AND DESCRIPTION 20cm. Size and plumage similar to that of Green Sandpiper, but longer legged and more delicate. Upperparts mottled brownish-grey with distinct spotting and clear feather edges. Juvenile slightly darker.

VOICE A dry 'chiff if if'.

HABITAT Breeds on wetlands in taiga, and during migration found on mudflats and riverbanks in western and southern Europe.

FOOD AND HABITS Wades in shallow water, feeding on invertebrates and plants. Nest a grassy scrape well hidden on the ground.

Juvenile

Adult summer

Green Sandpiper
Tringa ochropus

SIZE AND DESCRIPTION 22cm. Medium-sized and relatively robust sandpiper with distinctly contrasting plumage. Upperparts very dark, underparts white with a strongly separated dark breast. Juvenile more heavily speckled than adult.

VOICE Flight call 'tluit-uit-uit'; warning call 'tip tip'; song 'tloo-i tlui'.

HABITAT Mainly passage migrant in northern Europe, including Britain, with a few wintering in southern Britain. Occurs in all types of water body during migration. Breeds in damp forests near fresh water.

FOOD AND HABITS Feeds on invertebrates, as well as plant fragments. Often nests high in trees in abandoned nests of passerine birds.

Juvenile

Adult summer

Common Sandpiper
Actitis hypoleucos

SIZE AND DESCRIPTION 20cm. Small wader with brown upperparts, white underparts, white sides to the rump and tail, and a white wingbar.
VOICE Call in flight 'twee-wee-wee'. Song more melodious.
HABITAT Upland streams and lochs. In non-breeding season occurs on passage on inland waters such as reservoirs and sewage farms, and in coastal areas.
FOOD AND HABITS Eats mainly invertebrates, and some plant matter. Flicks tail. Nests in a shallow scrape on the ground.

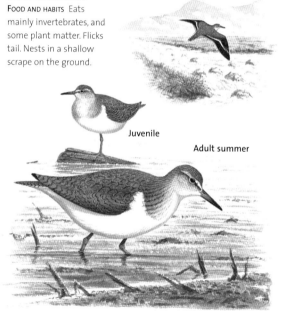

Juvenile

Adult summer

Curlew
Numenius arquata

Adult

SIZE AND DESCRIPTION 54cm. Largest wader, with a very long decurved bill. Plumage streaked brown. Bigger and more robust than Whimbrel. White 'V' shape on rump shows in flight.

VOICE Distinctive liquid call, 'coor-wee'.

HABITAT Breeds on moors and wet meadows, and winters on mudflats and fields, often on coasts. Resident in Britain.

FOOD AND HABITS Eats mainly small invertebrates, fish and plant matter. Long bill enables it to probe mud and sand deeply. Occurs in flocks outside breeding season, but feeds more separately. Nest a grassy cup well hidden on the ground.

Whimbrel
Numenius phaeopus

SIZE AND DESCRIPTION 41cm. Smaller and more slender than Curlew, with a shorter bill and a markedly striped face, pale crown stripe and dark stripe above the eye. White 'V' shape on rump shows in flight.

HABITAT Mostly a passage migrant to Britain, stopping on shores and coasts en route to wintering grounds further south.

FOOD AND HABITS Eats mostly molluscs, worms and crustaceans. Nests in a well-hidden grassy cup on the ground.

VOICE Liquid bubbling call.

Adult

Black-tailed Godwit
Limosa limosa

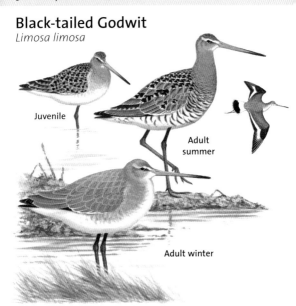

Juvenile

Adult
summer

Adult winter

SIZE AND DESCRIPTION 41cm. Breeding bird has a rufous-coloured breast. Colour outside breeding season grey-brown. In flight, a broad white wingbar and a white band on the tail above a black band distinguish it from Bar-tailed Godwit.

VOICE Call in flight 'wicka-wicka-wicka'. Song 'crweetuu'.

HABITAT Breeds on grassland and flood meadows. Winters in sheltered coastal areas in southern and western Europe. In Britain a scarce breeder in East Anglia and a widespread winter visitor.

FOOD AND HABITS Feeds mostly on insects and larvae; also molluscs and worms. Nest a cup well hidden in a tussock.

Bar-tailed Godwit
Limosa lapponica

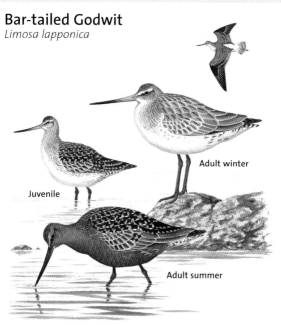

Adult winter

Juvenile

Adult summer

SIZE AND DESCRIPTION 37cm. Shorter legged and more robust than Black-tailed Godwit. In flight shows a distinct white rump and a barred tail.
VOICE Flight call nasal, similar to Knot's.
HABITAT Breeds in Scandinavia and on tundra. Winters on tidal mudflats and sandy shores from Britain southwards.
FOOD AND HABITS Probes mud for crabs, shrimps and marine worms in winter; insects taken mainly in summer. Nest a well-concealed scrape on the ground.

Turnstone
Arenaria interpres

Adult winter

Juvenile

Adult summer

Size and description 23cm. Boldly marked; looks blacks and white. Short and slightly upturned bill. Rufous markings in breeding plumage give it a tortoiseshell appearance.

Voice Variety of calls; typically short and nasal.

Habitat Breeds on stony tundra and along coasts. Winters along rocky coasts and breakwaters from Britain to Mediteranean.

Food and habits Diet is mainly insects, molluscs and crustaceans, which it finds by using its bill to overturn pebbles, and pieces of seaweed. Nest a shallow scrape well hidden on the ground.

Ruff
Philomachus pugnax

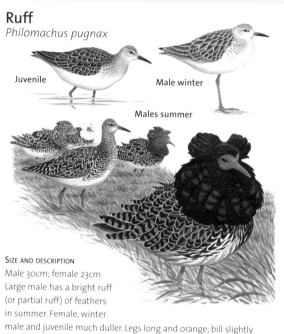

Juvenile

Male winter

Males summer

SIZE AND DESCRIPTION
Male 30cm; female 23cm.
Large male has a bright ruff
(or partial ruff) of feathers
in summer. Female, winter
male and juvenile much duller. Legs long and orange; bill slightly
decurved, and orange and black in male, blackish in female.

VOICE Usually silent.

HABITAT Coastal lagoons and inland marshes. Summer visitor to
northern Europe, where it breeds on tundra and marshland. Resident
year-round or winter visitor in south.

FOOD AND HABITS Diet is mainly insects, crustaceans, molluscs,
amphibians, small fish, and cereals and aquatic plants. Nest a deep
cup well hidden in grass.

Common Snipe
Gallinago gallinago

Adult

SIZE AND DESCRIPTION 27cm. Wader
most likely to be seen when flushed, flying off in a zigzag fashion.
Extremely long bill, striped yellow, and dark brown head and upperparts.
VOICE Hoarse cry when flushed.
HABITAT Breeds on flood meadows and moors, and winters on marshes
and wetlands in southern and western Europe.
FOOD AND HABITS Eats mainly worms; also molluscs, insects and
other invertebrates. Display flight involves a 45-degree
dive, with a bleating noise caused by air rushing
through outspread tail feathers. Nest a deep
cup well hidden in grass.

▶ SIMILAR SPECIES **Jack Snipe** (*Lymnocryptes minimus*)
At 19cm much smaller than
Common Snipe, with a
squatter shape, shorter legs
and a dark crown lacking a
pale central stripe. Breeds on
moors and marshes in north.
Winters in wet meadows in
southern and western Europe.

Adult

Woodcock
Scolopax rusticola

Adult

Size and description 34cm. Steep pale forehead, long bill, laterally striped crown, and marbled brown and buff upperparts. Most likely to be seen in display flight, 'roding', at dawn and dusk.

Voice Call given in display flight, a croak followed by 'tsiwick'.

Habitat Woodland with wet swampy areas and open glades and rides, as well as dense undergrowth cover. Summer visitor to north-east Europe. Winters south to Italy.

Food and habits Diet mostly worms, and also insects and larvae, seeds and grass. Crepuscular. Nest a scrape in leaf litter on the ground.

Red-necked Phalarope *Phalaropus lobatus*

Length 18cm. Graceful, with brick-red markings around the head in breeding plumage, and a white throat and belly. Non-breeding birds basically grey striped with white above, and white below. Breeds in ponds and tundra in northern Europe. In Britain small breeding population in Shetland and Hebrides; rare migrant elsewhere. Phalaropes feed by swimming on water, spinning round and picking up flies.

Adult winter

Female summer

Juvenile

Grey Phalarope *Phalaropus fulicarius*

Length 23cm. Similar to Red-necked, but slightly heavier and with a thicker bill. Breeding birds have a rusty-red throat and belly, black cap and white eye patch. Non-breeding birds grey above, white below. In Europe breeds only in Iceland. Winters in south Atlantic and scarce migrant to North Sea and Atlantic coasts, and occasionally inland.

Female summer

Juvenile

Adult winter

Great Skua
Stercorarius skua

Juvenile

Adult

Size and description 54 cm. Large thick-set skua that appears dark brown overall. Sexes are similar, and amount of brown in plumage differs. Large white crescent on upper- and underwing visible in flight.

Voice Call a low 'tok'.

Habitat Breeds in colonies on North Atlantic coasts, and winters at sea. Breeds north Scotland; passage migrant elsewhere in Britain.

Food and habits Harasses other birds into dropping or regurgitating food (klepto-parasitism). Will dive at intruders on its breeding grounds. Nest a bulky grass cup on the ground.

Arctic Skua
Sterocarius parasiticus

Adult dark morph

Juvenile

Adult light morph

SIZE AND DESCRIPTION 40cm. Size of a Common Gull, and the most common of the skuas. Occurs as a dark and pale morph, with brown or whitish underparts, as well as an intermediate variant. More buoyant and graceful flight than that of Great Skua.

VOICE Call a meowing 'aag-eeoo'.

HABITAT Summer visitor that breeds colonially on northern coasts, islands and tundra, and is migrant elsewhere.

FOOD AND HABITS Summer diet consists mostly of birds, small mammals and insects. Winter diet comprises fish, which are usually taken by piracy from other birds. Nest a grass cup on the ground.

Pomarine Skua
Stercorarius pomarinus

Adult dark morph

Juvenile

Adult light morph

SIZE AND DESCRIPTION 46cm. Occurs in a dark and light morph. Juvenile brown and barred. Breeding birds have central tail feathers elongated and twisted by 90 degrees, shaped like spoons.

VOICE Alarm call low 'geck'.

HABITAT Breeds in tundra. Passage migrant on North Sea and Atlantic coasts, including British coasts.

FOOD AND HABITS Eats lemmings, eggs and birds in summer, fish in winter, sometimes also stealing or scavenging.

SIMILAR SPECIES Long-tailed Skua (*S. longicaudus*). At 38cm long the smallest skua. Very long tail in breeding birds due to extended central tail feathers. Adult only occurs in a pale morph. Habitat and distribution as for Pomarine Skua.

Kittiwake
Rissa tridactyla

Adult

Juvenile

Size and description 41cm. Small gull with a grey back and wings, white head and underparts, dark eye, yellow bill and black legs. Solid black wingtips separate it from Common Gull, which has white 'windows'. Juvenile has a dark 'W' shape across wingspan.

Voice Calls its own name, 'kitt-ee-wayke'.

Habitat Breeds on cliffs in northern Europe, but otherwise almost entirely marine.

Food and habits Feeds on fish, worms, molluscs and crustaceans. Nests in colonies on cliff ledges.

Black-headed Gull
Chroicocephalus ridibundus

First winter

Adult winter

First summer

Adult summer

SIZE AND DESCRIPTION 37cm. In winter the head is white with a grey-brown crescent behind the eye. Breeding birds have a chocolate-brown head. Bill is red and finer than bills of most other European gulls.

VOICE Noisy when in flocks. Calls include a strident 'kee-yah'.

HABITAT Breeds in colonies on moorland bogs, freshwater marshes and lakes, and in reed beds across northern Europe. In winter common on ploughed fields and coasts, and in town parks, playing fields and large gardens.

FOOD AND HABITS Feeds on seeds and invertebrates, and scavenges in rubbish. Nest a large mound of flotsam and grass erected on the ground.

First summer

Juvenile

Adult summer

◀ **SIMILAR SPECIES Little Gull** (*Hydrocoloeus minutus*) At 26cm the smallest British gull. Adult in breeding plumage like a tiny Black-headed Gull. Juvenile has a blackish cap and a spot behind the eye. Breeds north-eastern Europe. Winters on coasts from Britain south to Mediterranean.

Mediterranean Gull *Larus melanocephalus*

Length 39cm. Similar to Black-
headed Gull but larger and
stockier, with a heavier bill.
Black hood in breeding birds
extends far down the nape;
patch behind and above the
eye in winter. Scarce in Britain
except in some sites in
southern England.

Adult winter

First winter

Glaucous Gull *Larus hyperboreus*

Length 65cm. White-winged gull
from the Arctic similar to a large
and powerful light-coloured
Herring Gull with a heavy bill.
Winters in north Atlantic south
to Britain and northern France.
In Britain most regular in north
and west.

Adult winter

**Adult
summe**

Iceland Gull *Larus glaucoides*

Length 55cm. Arctic gull almost
identical in all forms to
Glaucous Gull, but more
slender and delicate, and with
a 'kinder' face due to a more
rounded head and smaller bill.
Breeds in Greenland. Winters in
North Atlantic south to Britain.

Adult winter

Adult summer

Common Gull
Larus canus

Adult summer

Second winter

First winter

Adult winter

First winter

SIZE AND DESCRIPTION 41cm.
Resembles a small Herring Gull,
but the legs are yellow-green
and the bill lacks a red spot.
Grey upperparts, white below,
black wingtips and a 'kind'
facial expression. Juvenile
is streaked brown.

VOICE Higher pitched
than that of large gulls.

HABITAT Coasts; breeds
on moorland and
freshwater lochs. Mainly
resident in Britain, with
winter visitors from
northern Europe. After breeding many birds move south.

FOOD AND HABITS Feeds on earthworms, insects, seeds, small mammals,
birds and marine invertebrates. Nesl a grassy cup on the ground.

Herring Gull
Larus argentatus

Adult

Second winter

Juvenile

SIZE AND DESCRIPTION 61cm. Silver-grey upperparts, black wingtips, white head and underparts, yellow bill with a red spot, and pink legs. In winter the head and neck are streaked brown.

VOICE Wide variety of wailing calls. Loudest is 'kyow-kyow-kyow'.

HABITAT Coasts and inshore waters. In northern Europe abundant on coasts, and common inland in winter. Breeding increasingly inland.

FOOD AND HABITS Diet includes fish, crustaceans, carrion and birds. Nest a bulky mound of flotsam and grass.

SIMILAR SPECIES Yellow-legged Gull (*L. michahellis*). 55cm long. Similar to Herring Gull, but looks heavier with longer wings, and has a heavier bill and longer legs, yellow in adult; adult darker grey above. In Britain occurs in southern England, breeding rarely on coast.

Lesser Black-backed Gull
Larus fuscus

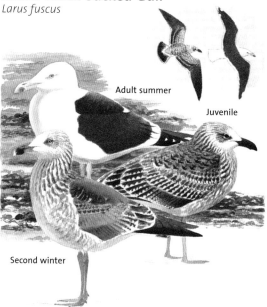

Adult summer

Juvenile

Second winter

SIZE AND DESCRIPTION 55cm. Dark grey back, white head and underparts, yellow bill with a red spot, and yellow legs. Juvenile brown, slightly darker than Herring Gull.

VOICE Loud calls, deeper than Herring Gull's.

HABITAT Coasts and sea. May breed on inland fresh waters.

FOOD AND HABITS Eats almost anything, including fish, small mammals, birds and their eggs, and carrion. May feed at rubbish tips. Nest a bulky mound of flotsam and grass.

Great Black-backed Gull
Larus marinus

Adult summer

Juvenile

Second winter

SIZE AND DESCRIPTION 72cm. Very large gull with black upperparts, a white head and underparts, a yellow bill with a red spot, and pink legs. Juvenile is brown.

VOICE Deep hoarse calls, 'uk-uk-uk'.

HABITAT Coasts and islands during breeding season. At other times also on estuaries and inland fresh waters.

FOOD AND HABITS Eats a wide variety of creatures, including fish, birds, mammals and carrion. May feed at rubbish tips. Nest built from flotsam and seaweed on a ledge.

Sandwich Tern
Sterna sandvicensis

Adult winter

Adult summer

Juvenile

SIZE AND DESCRIPTION 41cm. Large tern with pale plumage, rather short black legs, and a long and slender black bill. Breeding adults have a black crown with a shaggy crest, and a yellow tip to the bill. White forehead in winter.

VOICE Distinctive harsh 'kirrick'.

HABITAT Nests in enormous crowded colonies on sand or shingle banks along coasts. Winters in Mediterranean and further south.

FOOD AND HABITS Eats fish and other marine invertebrates. Nest a simple scrape in sand.

Common Tern
Sterna hirundo

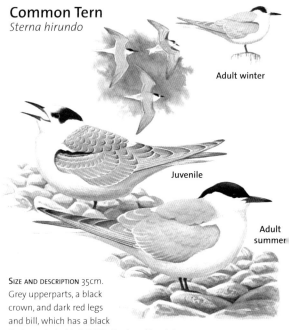

Adult winter

Juvenile

Adult summer

Size and description 35cm.
Grey upperparts, a black
crown, and dark red legs
and bill, which has a black
tip. Long forked tail. White forehead in winter.

Voice Call is a strident 'keeyah' and 'wik-kik-kik'.

Habitat Breeds on islands and inshore waters near low-lying coasts
and gravel pits. On passage occurs on lakes and inland waters. Mostly
a summer visitor, wintering outside Europe.

Food and habits Eats fish, worms, insects, molluscs and crustaceans.
Often dives for fish. Nests on dunes, salt marshes and shingle banks,
in colonies or as single pairs.

Arctic Tern
Sterna paradisaea

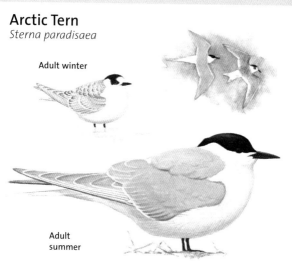

Adult winter

Adult summer

SIZE AND DESCRIPTION 35cm. Breeds mostly by coast in northern Britain. Elsewhere generally seen on passage. Similar to Common Tern, but with a blood-red bill. In winter has a white forehead with a black bill. Tends to have longer tail streamers.

VOICE Calls similar to those of Common Tern; also a high whistling 'kee, kee'.

HABITAT More maritime than Common Tern. Breeds in colonies along north European coasts. Winters off Africa.

FOOD AND HABITS Eats fish, insects, molluscs and crustaceans. Nest a shallow scrape in grass or sand.

Little Tern
Sternula albifrons

Adult winter

Juvenile

Adult summer

SIZE AND DESCRIPTION 23cm. Smallest of the black-capped 'white' terns. The tail is short and barely forked, and the wings are narrow. Breeding adult has a neat white forehead, yellow bill with a black tip, and orange legs. Winter adult and juvenile are duller.

VOICE Chattering calls.

HABITAT Breeds on flat sandy and shingly coastal beaches, and inland in continental Europe on stony lakes and rivers. Summer visitor to northern Europe.

FOOD AND HABITS Diet consists of small fish and invertebrates. Often hovers, employing very rapid wingbeats, before plunge-diving. Nesting birds on beaches are sensitive to disturbance, so decreasing where it is not fully protected.

Black Tern *Chlidonias niger*

Length 23cm. Marsh terns like this species
have shorter tails and broader wings than 'sea'
terns, and pick insects and larvae from the
water's surface rather
than plunge-diving.
Breeding plumage is
sooty black with paler
wings and a white
undertail, turning blotchy
in summer. Breeds
colonially on freshwater inland swamps
and marshes in southern, central and eastern
Europe. Winters outside Europe. In Britain
uncommon, occurring mainly in south.

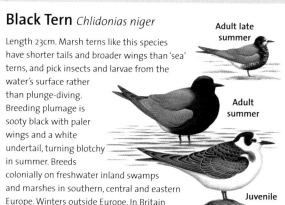

Adult late
summer

Adult
summer

Juvenile

Roseate Tern *Sterna dougallii*

Length 38cm. Similar to Common and Arctic Terns, but rarer. Breeding
birds have an almost black bill with a flush of red at the base. The
breast may have a pinkish (roseate) flush. Breeds very locally on coasts
of Britain, Ireland and north-west France. Winters in Africa.

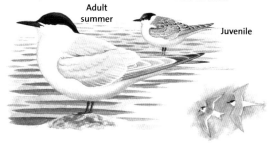

Adult
summer

Juvenile

Razorbill
Alca torda

Adult summer

Adult winter

SIZE AND DESCRIPTION 41cm. A black-and-white bird with a strong vertically flattened black bill. Juvenile and non-breeding birds have a white throat.

VOICE Makes a whirring sound and growls.

HABITAT Breeds on sea cliffs in northern Europe; winters at sea.

FOOD AND HABITS Diet almost entirely marine creatures. Fish are caught by diving from the water's surface and pursuing prey underwater by flapping the wings like flippers. Flight fast and whirring, usually low over the water. Breeds in colonies on rocky coasts with cliffs.

Common Guillemot
Uria aalge

Adult summer 'bridled' form

Adult summer

Adult winter

SIZE AND DESCRIPTION 43cm. The most common auk in Europe. Has short stubby wings, pied plumage and short legs. Upperparts are black/brown. Some birds have a white line over the eye and are known as 'bridled'. In winter the throat is white.

VOICE Call is a caw, 'aargh'.

HABITAT Breeds on sea cliffs in northern and western Europe, otherwise totally marine in North Sea and Atlantic.

FOOD AND HABITS Eats fish and other marine animals. Lays eggs on narrow cliff ledges. Colonies can comprise many thousands of pairs.

Puffin
Fratercula arctica

SIZE AND DESCRIPTION 30cm. Instantly recognizable by the bright bill and clown-like face markings. Smaller than Razorbill and Guillemot. In winter the bill is smaller and greyer, and the face is smudged.
VOICE Growling 'aar'.
HABITAT Breeds on clifftops and islands with grassy slopes in north-west Europe. Far out at sea during winter.
FOOD AND HABITS Eats mainly fish, especially sand-eels, and capable of holding several at a time in its notched bill. Highly gregarious, nesting in huge colonies. Nests in burrows or rocky crevices.

Adult winter

Adult summer

Black Guillemot *Cepphus grylle*

Length 35cm. Similar in shape to Guillemot, but much smaller. Breeding plumage distinctive, velvety black with red feet and a white wing patch. Non-breeding plumage variable but whiter, retaining the white wing patch. Displays with a high-pitched cricket-like 'siirrrrp'. Breeds in crevices and caves on rocky coasts in north of Britain and in Ireland.

Adult summer

Adult winter

Little Auk *Alle alle*

Length 20cm. Starling-sized auk that is dumpy and black above and white below, and has a whirring flight, often in flocks. Breeds at edge of Arctic; winters in northern north Atlantic. In Britain occurs on coasts in winter; may occur in large numbers off east coast.

Adult winter

Feral Pigeon *Columba livia* var. *domestica*

Rock Dove *Columba livia*

Rock Dove

Feral pigeons

SIZE AND DESCRIPTION 33cm.
With black wingbars
and a white rump, many
feral pigeons resemble
the Rock Doves from which they originate. However, colours vary from
white to very dark grey, and some may be pale fawn.

VOICE A soft cooing.

HABITAT Feral pigeon common in Europe in towns and cities, where it
breeds on buildings. Rock Dove locally common in mountains and on
rocky coasts, particularly in southern Europe. In Britain local on coasts
in western Scotland and western Ireland.

FOOD AND HABITS Seeds, grain and discarded human food. Rock Dove
nests in hollows and crevices, and on rock ledges.

Stock Dove
Columba oenas

Adults

SIZE AND DESCRIPTION 30cm. Smaller and less chunky than Woodpigeon, with a noticeable black trailing edge to its black-tipped wings. Lacks the wingbars and white rump of feral pigeon.

VOICE A monotonously repeated 'roo-roo-oo'.

HABITAT Woods and farmland, parks and gardens. Breeds across Europe. Absent from Iceland.

FOOD AND HABITS Feeds on seeds and grain, often in flocks with Woodpigeons. Nests in a hollow tree or burrow.

Woodpigeon
Columba palumbus

Adult

Juvenile

SIZE AND DESCRIPTION 41cm. Largest European pigeon. Adult has white rings around neck, and a white bar across each wing. Wings make a clattering sound on take-off and landing.

VOICE A soft, often repeated 'coo-coo-coo-cu-coo'.

HABITAT Woodland, farmland, parks and gardens across Europe.

FOOD AND HABITS Eats seeds, berries and beechmast. Feeds in flocks throughout winter. Nest a platform of twigs in a tree or bush.

Collared Dove
Streptopelia decaocto

SIZE AND DESCRIPTION 32cm. Slimmer than other pigeons. Back is brown-buff, head and underparts pinkish-brown. Black ring around nape of neck, and wings with whitish undersides.

VOICE A rapidly repeated 'koo-koo, koo'.

HABITAT Towns, gardens and farmland with hedges. Has spread across Europe from Asia.

FOOD AND HABITS Feeds on seeds and grain. Frequent bird-table visitor. Large flocks assemble at grain stores. Nest a platform of twigs in a tree or bush, or on a ledge.

Adult

Juvenile

Turtle Dove
Streptopelia turtur

Juvenile

Adult

SIZE AND DESCRIPTION 26cm. Adult
rich bronze with the back and
wings mottled with brown and
black. Underparts pinkish-buff shading to white on the belly. Head
and neck grey with chequered black-and-white collar patches.
VOICE Distinctive gentle purring, 'turrr, turrr', from which the common
name of the species is derived.
HABITAT Woodland and farmland with hedges and scrub. Breeds over
much of Europe except far north. Winters in tropical Africa.
FOOD AND HABITS European population has declined substantially, partly
because of changing farming practices resulting in scarcity of plants
on which it feeds, and partly due to shooting of migrating birds in
Mediterranean. Nest a platform of twigs in a bush.

Ring-necked Parakeet
Psittacula krameri

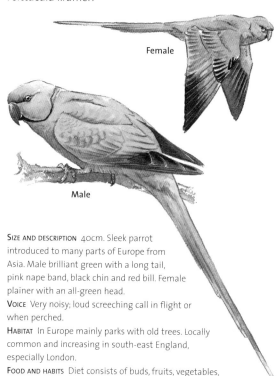

Female

Male

SIZE AND DESCRIPTION 40cm. Sleek parrot introduced to many parts of Europe from Asia. Male brilliant green with a long tail, pink nape band, black chin and red bill. Female plainer with an all-green head.

VOICE Very noisy; loud screeching call in flight or when perched.

HABITAT In Europe mainly parks with old trees. Locally common and increasing in south-east England, especially London.

FOOD AND HABITS Diet consists of buds, fruits, vegetables, nuts, berries and seeds. Nests mainly in tree hollows.

Cuckoo
Cuculus canorus

Rufous female

Juvenile

Male

SIZE AND DESCRIPTION
34cm. Slim-looking
bird with long swept-
back wings and a long
rounded tail. Grey
with a pale, barred breast. Some females may be rufous. Juvenile
barred, brown, with a white patch on the nape.

VOICE Male gives well-known 'cuckoo' call; female has a bubbling trill.

HABITAT Wide range of habitats, including moorland, heathland, open
woodland, parks and large gardens. Summer visitor to Europe except
Iceland, arriving from Africa in April and leaving in late summer.

FOOD AND HABITS Eats insects and is capable of swallowing hairy
caterpillars. Females lay eggs in other birds' nests.

Barn Owl
Tyto alba

Adult

SIZE AND DESCRIPTION 34cm. Golden-spangled back, heart-shaped pale face and white underparts. Longer wings and legs than Tawny Owl.

VOICE Call is a screech; also makes hissing and snoring sounds.

HABITAT Fields, meadows and marshes; needs open country with rough grassland for hunting.

FOOD AND HABITS Feeds mainly on rodents, especially rats and voles. Often nests in buildings, usually old barns and farm outhouses. Largely nocturnal, and often seen in car headlights as it searches verges for prey.

Long-eared Owl *Asio otus*

Length 34cm. Cryptic brown plumage, long ear-tufts usually flattened in flight and an orange iris. Underparts more densely streaked than those of Short-eared Owl, and wingtips and tail more finely barred. Voice a long low hoot during breeding season; juvenile utters a high-pitched 'squeaky gate' call. Breeds mainly in coniferous forests across Europe, often nesting in old crows' nests. In Britain uncommon and local.

Adult

Short-eared Owl *Asio flammeus*

Length 37cm. Paler than Long-eared Owl with less obvious ear-tufts and yellow eyes ringed with black feathers. In flight shows more uniform dark wingtips, white trailing edges to the wings and coarse barring on tail. Voice a hollow 'boo boo boo boo' in breeding season; call 'tchee-op'. Occurs on moors, heaths, wet meadows and open areas, nesting on the ground. Winters in southern and western Europe. In Britain breeds in north and is widespread in winter.

Adult

Tawny Owl
Strix aluco

Juveniles

Adult

Size and

description 38cm.
Woodland owl more
likely to be heard than
seen as it is almost entirely
nocturnal. Brown plumage, broad rounded wings, feathered feet,
dark eyes and a round face mask.

Voice Song consists of familiar hooting, 'hooh, hu-huhu hooh', call
a sharp 'kewick'.

Habitat Deciduous woodland, forests and parks with mature trees
across Europe except north and Ireland.

Food and habits Mostly eats small mammals such as Wood Mice,
and small birds. Nests in holes in trees. May be betrayed at roost
in daylight by small birds mobbing it.

Little Owl
Athene noctua

Adult

Juvenile

Hunting

Size and description 22cm. More likely to be seen in daylight than Tawny or Barn Owls. Yellow eyes, a 'fierce' expression, long legs and brown upper parts spotted with white. Flight a fast flap and glide.

Voice Call a ringing 'kiew, kiew'.

Habitat Open country and farmland with scattered trees, and open woodland. An introduced species now widespread in much of Europe, including Britain, except north and north-west.

Food and habits Diet is chiefly large insects and other invertebrates, such as worms. Nests in holes in trees.

European Nightjar
Caprimulgus europaeus

Female

Male

Male

SIZE AND DESCRIPTION 27cm. Species with cryptic camouflage resembling bark and leaves that allows bird to conceal itself very well on the ground or on a branch. Male shows bold white flashes on the wingtips and tip of tail during flight, which is falcon-like.

VOICE Sings at night with a regular deep, rather mechanical churring. Call a frog-like 'kruu-ik'; in flight 'fiorr-fiorrr-fiorr' with clapping of wings.

HABITAT Breeds on heaths and moors, and in forest edges and clearings. Summer visitor to much of Europe except far north. Winters in Africa.

FOOD AND HABITS Feeds on insects caught on the wing. Nests in a well-concealed simple scrape on the ground.

Common Swift
Apus apus

SIZE AND DESCRIPTION 17cm. Long and narrow crescent-shaped wings, a torpedo-shaped body, a short forked tail and very short legs. Plumage is dark brown with a pale throat.

VOICE Shrill monotone scream, often uttered by tight flocks flying around buildings at roof-top height.

HABITAT Breeds in towns and villages, but feeds in the sky, often several kilometres from nest sites. Summer visitor to northern Europe (except Iceland), usually arriving in May and leaving in August.

FOOD AND HABITS Adapted to feed on high-flying insects, which it catches in its wide gaping mouth. Shuffles around nest site on short legs. Most of its life is spent on the wing.

Juvenile

Adult

Kingfisher
Alcedo atthis

Family

Female

Male

Size and description 18cm. Although
brightly coloured, Kingfishers are
well camouflaged when perched
among leaves. Bill is black, but female has a reddish base to lower
mandible. Juvenile has a pale spot at the tip of its bill.

Voice Distinctive whistle, 'tee-eee' and 'tsee'.

Habitat Rivers, streams and lakes. Visits garden ponds to take small
ornamental fish.

Food and habits Fish are the main food. Hunts by diving into water
from a perch, or by hovering and then diving. Excavates breeding
tunnels in steep sandbanks.

Hoopoe
Upupa epops

Adults

Adult

SIZE AND DESCRIPTION 27cm. Upperparts
sandy-fawn with black-and-white
barred wings and tail. Bill curves
downwards. Crest is raised and
fanned when the bird lands, or when it
is startled. Wings are broad and flight is
flappy, often low over the ground. Walks
jerkily with a Starling-like gait.

VOICE A repeated 'poo-poo-poo'.

HABITAT Gardens, vineyards, olive groves,
and farmland with bushes. Visits
northern Europe in late April to
September, moving south to North
Africa and southern Spain in winter.

FOOD AND HABITS Feeds on insects,
worms and small reptiles. Nests in
tree hollows, stables, rock piles or
earth heaps.

Green Woodpecker
Picus viridis

Male

Female

Juvenile

SIZE AND DESCRIPTION 33cm. Green plumage, but with a distinctive yellow rump and a red cap. Juvenile is speckled and appears more grey. Flight is deeply undulating. A pale eye and black face and moustachial stripe give the bird a 'fierce' appearance. Male has a red centre to his moustachial stripe, while female's is black. Undulating flight.

VOICE An unmistakable shrill laughing call. Rarely drums.

HABITAT Deciduous and mixed forest edges, woodland, farmland, parkland and large gardens.

FOOD AND HABITS Feeds on insect grubs and ants, for which it probes soil and rotten wood. Often seen feeding on large open areas of grass. Nests in a hole made in a tree.

Lesser Spotted Woodpecker
Dendrocopos minor

Length 26cm. Miniature version of Great
Spotted Woodpecker, size of a House Sparrow.
Fine white barring on the back, and longer and
more high-pitched drumming than that of
Great. Lives in deciduous forests, often close to
wetlands. In Britain occurs in southern England
and Wales, and declining.

Male

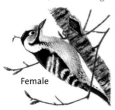

Female

Juvenile

Wryneck *Jynx torquilla*

Length 17cm. Small woodpecker
more often seen on branches than
clinging to tree trunks. Cryptic
plumage gives good camouflage.
Does not drum. Occurs in open
forests, orchards and old parks, and
feeds on ants. Does not excavate its
own nest hole. Winters in Africa –
the only migratory woodpecker
species. In Britain scarce on south
and east coasts; a few possibly
breeding in Scottish Highlands.

Adults

Great Spotted Woodpecker
Dendrocopos major

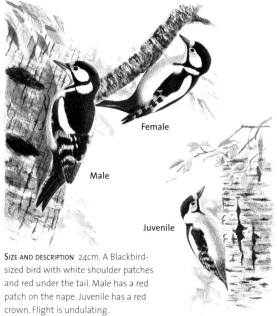

Female

Male

Juvenile

SIZE AND DESCRIPTION 24cm. A Blackbird-sized bird with white shoulder patches and red under the tail. Male has a red patch on the nape. Juvenile has a red crown. Flight is undulating.

VOICE A short sharp 'tchak' call, which may be repeated at 1-second intervals. In spring drums very fast on rotten branches.

HABITAT All kinds of woodland, large gardens and parks.

FOOD AND HABITS Insects and grubs, and conifer seeds in winter. Visits garden feeders. Also steals eggs and young from other birds' nests. Nests in a hole made in a tree.

Skylark
Alauda arvensis

Song flight

Adult winter

Adult summer

SIZE AND DESCRIPTION 18cm. Streaked brown upperparts, short crest not always obvious, white outer tail feathers. Walks rather than hops. Towering and hovering song flight.

VOICE Lengthy warbling song delivered in flight as bird rises vertically, then drops through the air.

HABITAT Farmland, grassland, meadows and moorland throughout most of Europe.

FOOD AND HABITS Eats insects, worms and seeds. Nests on the ground. Flocks in winter, when numbers are swollen by European migrants. Nest a grassy cup well hidden on the ground. Common but declining.

Shore Lark *Eremophila alpestris*

Length 17cm. Breeding plumage includes black-and-yellow head pattern. Male develops two small feathered black ear-tufts, or 'horns', as he attains breeding plumage. Breeds on mountain meadows,

Adult winter

Male summer

tundra and fells; winters mainly on North Sea coasts; resident only in Balkans. In Britain scarce and mainly on east coast in late autumn and winter.

Woodlark *Lullula arborea*

Length 14cm. Slightly smaller than Skylark and with a shorter tail. Face and head have a much stronger pattern, with a conspicuous white stripe above the eye and a white patch on the leading edge of the outer wing. Occurs in mountain meadows and clearings, and on heathland, across Europe except far north. Uncommon in Britain; increasing in south.

Adult

Swallow
Hirundo rustica

Juvenile

Adult male

SIZE AND DESCRIPTION 19cm including tail of 3–6.5cm. Wings long and pointed, tail deeply forked. Pale cream underparts, dark blue wings and back, and a red throat with a blue-black neck band. Fast flight with powerful wingbeats.

VOICE High-pitched 'vit-vit' call in flight. Warning call for cats and other ground predators a sharp 'sifflit'; for birds of prey, 'flitt-flitt'. Song a rapid rattling twitter.

HABITAT Breeds in farmyards and small-village gardens with surrounding open country. Often seen near water. Summer visitor to northern Europe.

FOOD AND HABITS Feeds on insects, which it catches in flight by flying low over fields and water. Cup-shaped clay nest built in buildings.

Sand Martin
Riparia riparia

Adults

SIZE AND DESCRIPTION 12cm. Small brown bird with white underparts, a brown breast-band and a short forked tail.

VOICE Twittering song, not as musical as that of Swallow.

HABITAT Open country with fresh water. Summer visitor and migrant across Europe except far north.

FOOD AND HABITS Eats insects such as midges caught in flight. Nests colonially in burrows excavated in sandbanks. On migration may roost in large numbers in reed beds.

House Martin
Delichon urbica

Nesting

Adult

Juvenile

SIZE AND DESCRIPTION 14cm. Wings broader than Swallow's and forked tail shorter, giving a stubbier appearance. Rump white, and wings, head and tail dark blue. Flight more fluttery than Swallow's, with flaps often interspersed with glides. Underparts of juvenile usually duskier white than adult's.

VOICE Harsh twitter. Song a series of formless chirps.

HABITAT Breeds in colonies in towns and villages, and on cliffs. Summer visitor and migrant across Europe except far north. Winters in Africa.

FOOD AND HABITS Tends to feed on flying insects at greater altitude than Swallow. Rarely on the ground, except when collecting mud for nest. Builds rounded mud nest under protrusions on buildings, and sometimes cliffs.

Tree Pipit
Anthus trivialis

SIZE AND DESCRIPTION 15cm. Similar to Meadow Pipit, but slightly stockier, although best separated by voice. Walks rather than hops.

VOICE Call a drawn-out 'speez', given from a tree or in flight, steeply ascending then parachuting down.

HABITAT Meadowland and heathland with scattered trees. Summer visitor to Europe. Winters in Africa.

FOOD AND HABITS Feeds mainly on insects and spiders. Nest a grassy cup well hidden on the ground.

Male song flight

Adult

Meadow Pipit
Anthus pratensis

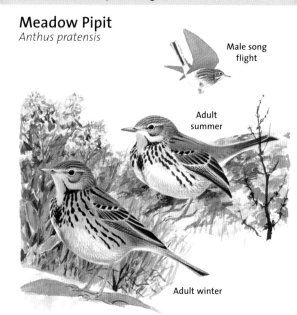

Male song flight

Adult summer

Adult winter

SIZE AND DESCRIPTION 15cm. Streaked brown upperparts; underparts spotted. Darker legs than Tree Pipit. Best identified by call.
VOICE Call 'pheet' uttered 1–5 times. Song given from perch or in display flight as it describes an arc from the ground.
HABITAT Open country, heathland, moorland and grassland. May be seen in lowlands or on coastal land in winter. Year-round resident, migrant or winter visitor in much of Europe.
FOOD AND HABITS Eats mostly insects; also spiders, earthworms and some seeds. Nests on the ground in a small depression.

Water Pipit *Anthus spinoletta*

Length 16cm. Similar build to Rock Pipit, but with brown upperparts and a white stripe above the eye and white outer tail feathers. Breeding birds have a pinkish unstreaked breast. Breeds in mountain meadows mainly in southern Europe. Call 'veest'; song similar to that of Meadow Pipit, but stronger. Winters in lowland wetlands and coasts from southern England to Mediterranean. Uncommon in Britain; mainly in south.

Adult summer

Adult winter

Rock Pipit *Anthus petrosus*

Length 16cm. Similar to Water Pipit, but with pale grey outer tail feathers. Plumage is uniform dusky brown with heavily mottled buff underparts. Call and song like that of Water Pipit. Found on rocky coasts of northern and western Europe, and relatively common on British coasts.

Adults

Grey Wagtail
Motacilla cinerea

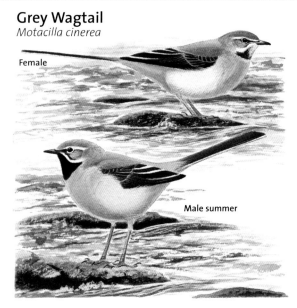

Female

Male summer

SIZE AND DESCRIPTION 19cm. Longest tailed of European wagtails. Grey above and lemon yellow below, with colour particularly strong under the tail, and pink legs. Summer adult male has a distinctive black throat. Tail is constantly wagging.

VOICE Call a sharp 'tzit'. Song a simple and metallic 'ziss-ziss-ziss'.

HABITAT Vicinity of running water, from mountain streams to towns. Occurs year-round throughout much of Europe; summer visitor to north and north-east.

FOOD AND HABITS Insectivorous; often chases insects over the water. Nest a grassy cup usually hidden in a cavity near water.

Pied & White Wagtails
Motacilla alba

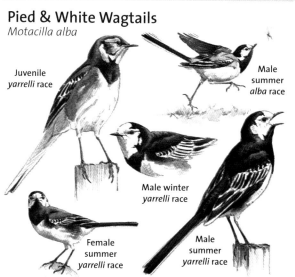

Juvenile *yarrelli* race

Male summer *alba* race

Male winter *yarrelli* race

Female summer *yarrelli* race

Male summer *yarrelli* race

SIZE AND DESCRIPTION 18cm. Male of British race (*M. a. yarrellii*) has a black back and wings, female a dark grey back. In continental race (*M. a. alba*), both male and female have a pale grey back. In flight, which is undulating, faint double wingbars can be seen.

VOICE Flight call a 'chissick', sometimes a 'chissick-ick'. Song plain and twittery.

HABITAT Towns, gardens and open habitats.

FOOD AND HABITS Runs rapidly after flying insects. On the ground its gait is rapid, and its head is moved backwards and forwards while wagging its tail. Prefers feeding on lawns and roofs, and in car parks and roads, where prey is easily spotted. In winter roosts in large flocks in warm places like factories. Nest a grassy cup in a cavity.

Yellow & Blue-headed Wagtails
Motacilla flava

SIZE AND DESCRIPTION 16cm. Several subspecies, with Yellow, *M. f. flavissima*, by far the most common in Britain. Head green with a yellow throat and supercilium; mantle a brighter yellow-green; slender black legs. Blue-headed *M. f. flava* male has a pale blue head.
VOICE Call a rich 'tseep'. Song a simple scratching 'sri'srit sri...'
HABITAT Meadows, farmland and marshes. *M. f. flavissima* breeds in Britain and on neighbouring European coasts from France to Norway. *M. f. flava* occurs on much of the Continent. Winters in Africa.
FOOD AND HABITS Insectivorous. Grassy cup nest well concealed on the ground. In decline since the 1980s, probably due to loss of habitat.

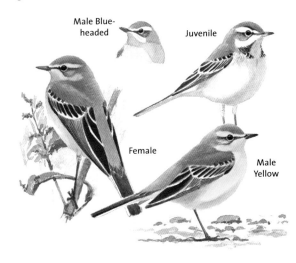

Male Blue-headed

Juvenile

Female

Male Yellow

Waxwing
Bombycilla garrulus

SIZE AND DESCRIPTION 20cm. Starling-sized bird with overall pinkish-brown plumage, a long crest, black chin and mask, and yellow-banded tail. Male is usually brighter in colour than female.

VOICE Call a soft sibilant trilling, 'sirrrr'. Song a slow and soft bell-like trill with rougher notes.

HABITAT In Europe breeds in far northern taiga with coniferous forests. In winter flocks to gardens and parks where there are berries south to Britain and the Balkans.

FOOD AND HABITS Feeds mainly on berries, supplemented by insects, particularly during breeding season.

Female

Male

Dipper
Cinclus cinclus

Juvenile

Adult

SIZE AND DESCRIPTION 19cm. Small plump bird with a Wren-like appearance. Adult has a white bib and a red-brown belly (black-brown belly in north European subspecies). Juvenile grey and barred all over.
VOICE Call a short 'zit'. Song a sweet soft warble.
HABITAT Fast-flowing freshwater rivers and streams, particularly in mountains, across much of Europe. In Britain fairly common in north and west.
FOOD AND HABITS Forages for small animals in streams and rivers. Unique among songbirds in its ability to dive into water and walk or fly along the bottom in search of food. Nest a grassy cup in the fork of a tree.

Wren
Troglodytes troglodytes

Nesting

SIZE AND DESCRIPTION 10cm. Tiny bird with a short
tail often held cocked above the back, a round body
and a short neck. The reddish-brown back is faintly
barred, as are the paler flanks. Narrow dark eyestripe and paler
stripe above the eye. Whirring flight, rather like that of a large bee.

VOICE Calls a repeated 'tic-tic' and metallic 'clink'. Song an amazingly
loud series of alternately sweet and rattling trills and warbles.

HABITAT Woodland with dense undergrowth, scrub, heathland,
gardens, parks and moorland in most of Europe.

FOOD AND HABITS Searches mouse-like for insects and spiders on
or near the ground. During cold winter nights flocks may roost
together. Nest a domed grassy structure well hidden in a hollow or
vegetation. Males may build several nests for females to select from.

Dunnock
Prunella modularis

Display

Juvenile

Adult

SIZE AND DESCRIPTION 14cm. Streaking and brown colouration give this bird a rather sparrow-like appearance, which is why it is often wrongly described as a Hedge Sparrow. It has a thin insect-picking bill, grey throat and face, and reddish-brown legs.

VOICE Alarm call a strong 'tiih'. Song clear and quite loud.

HABITAT Gardens, parks, open woodland, heathland, farmland and hedges over most of Europe.

FOOD AND HABITS An unobtrusive bird that scurries around on the ground, mouse-like, looking for seeds, berries, insects and other invertebrates. Nest a grass cup well hidden in a shrub.

Blackbird
Turdus merula

Juvenile

Female

Male

SIZE AND DESCRIPTION 25cm. The all-black male, with his yellow bill and yellow eyering, is unmistakable. The sooty-brown female, with a dark-streaked pale throat, and the gingery juvenile, may be confused with other thrushes, but they have a solid build and cock their tails when landing. First-winter males have all-dark bills.

VOICE Alarm call a harsh 'chack-aack-aack-aack', or a series of high metallic notes when going to roost or when a cat is seen. Song a rich melodic fluting, often rising to a crescendo.

HABITAT Woodland, parks, orchards and gardens across Europe.

FOOD AND HABITS Hops or walks over the ground, stopping and cocking its head to look for worms or other food. Takes a wide range of food, including insects, worms, fruits and berries.

Ring Ouzel
Turdus torquatus

Female

Male
summer

Male
winter

Size and description 24cm. Dull plumage, sooty black in male, sooty brown in female. White crescentic patch in male, often obscure in female and juvenile.

Voice Call an excitable 'tack tack'. Song melodious, with 2–4 repeated flute-like tones.

Habitat Breeds in forested fells in northern Europe, and mountainous conifer forests in central Europe. Winters in southern Europe, favouring lowland fields and forest edges.

Food and habits Omnivorous, consuming a wide range of insects, rodents, lizards and berries. Nest a neat cup in bushes or among rocks.

Fieldfare
Turdus pilaris

Adults

SIZE AND DESCRIPTION 26cm. Smaller than Mistle Thrush, but looks stockier. Grey head, red-brown back and apricot base to speckled breast. Longish tail, pale grey rump and white underwings show clearly in rather flapping flight.

VOICE Call a dry 'chack-chack-chack', like that of a Magpie. Song a tuneless chattering babble.

HABITAT Open forest, town parks, fields and gardens. Winter visitor or migrant to much of Europe; year-round in north-central areas; summer only in far north. In Britain breeds rarely in Scotland.

FOOD AND HABITS Feeds on worms, insects, berries and fruits. Fond of windfall fruits. Nest a grassy cup in the fork of a tree.

Redwing
Turdus iliacus

Adults

Size and description 21cm. Similar size to
Song Thrush, but with visibly larger
head. White stripe above the eye and
black-tipped yellow bill give it a striking appearance. Red patch under
the wing conspicuous in flight, which is fast and direct.
Voice Thin 'tseep' contact call. Alarm call hoarse and scolding. Song
variable, with loud fluted notes and prolonged twitters.
Habitat Fields, open woodland, parks and gardens. Summer visitor to
northern Europe, wintering in southern and western Europe.
Food and habits Feeds on worms, insects and berries. Nest a grassy
cup in a shrub or tree.

Song Thrush
Turdus philomelos

Adults

SIZE AND DESCRIPTION 23cm. Brown back and speckled creamy breast (speckles shaped like arrowheads, and more regular than those of Mistle Thrush). In flight, underwings show yellowish-orange. Flies rather jerkily.

VOICE Beautiful strong song with a variety of trilling and squeaky notes and frequent repetitions, often sung at dusk. Alarm call a series of sharp scolding notes.

HABITAT Woodland, parks and gardens across most of Europe.

FOOD AND HABITS Feeds on worms, insects, berries and snails. Sometimes in small flocks. Nest a mud-lined grassy cup in a shrub. Common but declining.

Mistle Thrush
Turdus viscivorus

SIZE AND DESCRIPTION 28cm. Large thrush with a comparatively longer tail than that of Song Thrush. White breast speckled with rounded blotchy spots. In flight white outer tail feathers and narrow white wingbars can be seen. Underwing is white. Stands in an upright posture. Flight more undulating than Song Thrush's.

VOICE Flight call a dry churring rattle. Song similar to Song Thrush's.

HABITAT Woodland, parks and gardens throughout Europe.

FOOD AND HABITS Eats worms, berries and insects. Feeds alongside other birds. Nest an untidy grass and leaf cup usually high up in tree canopy. Common but declining.

Adults

Goldcrest
Regulus regulus

SIZE AND DESCRIPTION 9cm. Tiny
with a greenish back and a
yellow crest that becomes
orange in male. Crest has a
black stripe on each side.
Face greyish with dark eyes
surrounded by very pale grey.
VOICE Very high-pitched thin
call of 3–4 syllables, 'see-see-
see'. Song high-pitched and
rhythmic, and ending with
a trill.
HABITAT Coniferous and mixed
woodland; often seen in yew
and cypress trees.
FOOD AND HABITS Feeds on tiny
insects and spiders on the
undersides of leaves. Nest
a mossy hammock high in
a tree.

Male

Female

Firecrest
Regulus ignicapilla

SIZE AND DESCRIPTION 9 cm. Similar to Goldcrest. In all plumages has
a black eyestripe and white supercilium.
VOICE Call slightly lower pitched than Goldcrest's, rising in pitch
when notes are consecutive. Song very high-pitched and ascending,
'si si-sisisisisihrr'.
HABITAT Coniferous and mixed woodland and parks; also more open
bushy places in winter. Occurs in much of central and western Europe.
In Britain scarce and local.
FOOD AND HABITS Feeds on insects. Nest as Goldcrest.

Juvenile

Male

Female

Willow Warbler
Phylloscopus trochilus

Adult

Juvenile

SIZE AND DESCRIPTION 11.5cm. Head, back and tail generally brownish-green; throat and eyebrow yellowish; legs usually pale brown. Primary feathers project beyond tertials.

VOICE Call a soft 'huitt' similar to Common Chiffchaff's. Song rather sad.

HABITAT Upland birchwoods and other deciduous woods, and parks and gardens. Occurs across much of Europe apart from south.

FOOD AND HABITS Feeds on insects found among leaves. Nest a grassy dome on or near the ground.

▶ **SIMILAR SPECIES Yellow-browed Warbler** (*P. inornatus*) 10 cm. Petite and agile bird. Moss-green above with two distinct yellow wingbars, a long supercilium and a diffuse crown-stripe. Vagrant to Britain, but increasing and sometimes wintering.

Common Chiffchaff
Phylloscopus collybita

Adults

Size and description 11cm. Small neat bird with a fine bill and thin legs.
Very similar to Willow Warbler. Primaries shorter. Legs usually dark
and bill even finer. Stripe above the eye less distinct, while darkish
patch beneath the eye emphasizes white eyering.

Voice Call a soft 'hueet'. Song a distinctively slow 'chiff-chaff-chiff-chaff'.

Habitat Open deciduous woodland with some scrub. Mainly summer
visitor to Britain, Scandinavia and central Europe.

Food and habits Similar to Willow Warbler.

Wood Warbler *Phylloscopus sibilatrix*

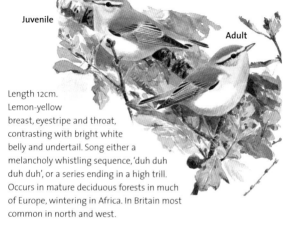

Juvenile

Adult

Length 12cm.
Lemon-yellow
breast, eyestripe and throat,
contrasting with bright white
belly and undertail. Song either a
melancholy whistling sequence, 'duh duh
duh duh', or a series ending in a high trill.
Occurs in mature deciduous forests in much
of Europe, wintering in Africa. In Britain most
common in north and west.

Grasshopper Warbler *Locustella naevia*

Length 13cm. Skulking brown warbler
streaked olive-brown above and with pale
underparts, often with unclear streaks
on the breast. Usually hides in thick low
vegetation, moving mouse-like on or
near the ground. Call a grasshopper-
like 'serrrrrrrrrrr' lasting for
minutes. Favours dense
cover in open areas.
Summer visitor to much of
Europe including Britain.

Adult

Reed Warbler
Acrocephalus scirpaceus

Adults

SIZE AND DESCRIPTION 13cm.
Small olive-brown warbler
with slight rufous tinge to
its upperparts. Buff-coloured
below. Rounded tail. Sexes look similar.

VOICE Monotonous churring song.

HABITAT Mainly reed beds. Summer visitor to Britain.

FOOD AND HABITS Eats water insects. In autumn feeds on berries, which
provide energy for its long migratory flight. Builds a nest of woven
grasses slung between reed stems. Common host to Cuckoo.

Sedge Warbler
Acrocephalus schoenobaenus

SIZE AND DESCRIPTION 13cm. Olive-brown streaked-backed warbler with a rounded tail and rufous-coloured rump. Conspicuous creamy-white stripe above the eye. Sexes look similar.

VOICE Loud, jumbly and scratchy song.

HABITAT Waterside vegetation near reed beds, rivers and lakes, and lowland marshes; also dry scrubby areas. Summer visitor to Britain, migrating to Africa in late summer.

FOOD AND HABITS Mainly eats insects; takes berries in autumn. Nests in rank vegetation.

Adult

Juvenile

Dartford Warbler *Sylvia undata*

13cm long. Tiny, with a very long tail. Male has a grey back and dark red-brown breast. Female is duller and browner. Soft grating 'chirr' call and scratchy song. On the Continent resident year-round in west, south-west and south, favouring gorse and heather heathland and scrub. In Britain quite common in suitable habitats in southern England and East Anglia.

Adult male

Cetti's Warbler *Cettia cetti*

14cm long. Small and skulking unstreaked warbler. Upperparts uniform brown, shading to buff on the breast sides and flanks, and to white on the belly. Tail brown and relatively long. Song a very loud and explosive burst of fruity metallic notes; call a sharp 'teck'. On the Continent resident mainly in south and south-west, favouring dense vegetation beside water. Colonized Britain in the 1970s and increasing.

Adult

Common Whitethroat
Sylvia communis

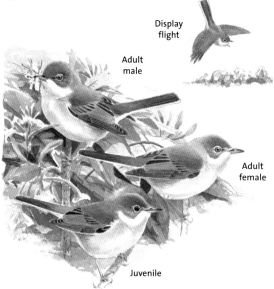

Display flight

Adult male

Adult female

Juvenile

SIZE AND DESCRIPTION 14cm. Male has a grey head, a bright white throat, brown upperparts and pale underparts. Female has a brown head. Tail long and slim.

VOICE Call a sharp 'tacc, tacc'. Song a rapid warble.

HABITAT Open woodland, gardens, hedgerows and scrub. Summer visitor to Britain.

FOOD AND HABITS Eats mainly insects, and some fruits and berries in autumn. Nests in brambles and low bushes not far from the ground.

Lesser Whitethroat
Sylvia curruca

Juvenile

Adult

Size and description 13 cm. Easy to distinguish from Common Whitethroat by duller brown back and wings, lacking any rufous colouration, bright white underparts and dark grey legs.

Voice Call an abrupt 'tack'. Song a simple brief warble ending with a repetitive single-note rattle.

Habitat Farmland with trees and hedges, woodland edges, parks, large gardens and scrub. Summer visitor to Britain.

Food and habits Insectivorous, but also takes berries and other soft fruits. Grass cup nest is built in a low shrub or brambles.

Blackcap
Sylvia atricapilla

Female

Male

SIZE AND DESCRIPTION 14cm. Male has a black cap; female's is red-brown. Cheeks are grey; upperparts dark grey-brown.

VOICE Warning call a harsh 'teck' and 'tack'ack'ack'. Sweet rich warbling song.

HABITAT Open woodland, shrubby areas with trees, and gardens. Mostly summer visitor to Britain; increasing numbers seen in winter.

FOOD AND HABITS Chiefly eats insects, and berries and fruits in late summer and autumn. Occasional visitor to bird tables. Nest a neat grass cup concealed low in bush.

Garden Warbler
Sylvia borin

Adults

SIZE AND DESCRIPTION 14cm. Inconspicuous little grey-brown warbler. Plumage uniform without any notable distinguishing feature. Round head, short bill.

VOICE Song most distinctive characteristic, a musical warble uttered from depths of cover.

HABITAT Deciduous and mixed woodland with dense undergrowth. Summer visitor to Britain.

FOOD AND HABITS Eats mostly insects in early summer; also berries and other fruits before autumn migration. Nests in brambles and bushes.

Pied Flycatcher
Ficedula hypoleuca

Female/juvenile

Male summer

SIZE AND DESCRIPTION 13cm. Breeding male has bold black-and-white plumage. Shorter tailed and more compact than Spotted Flycatcher, with a white wingbar. Constantly flicks its wings and tail.

VOICE Calls include a metallic 'whit'. Song quite shrill, 'zee-it, zee-it', interspersed with trills.

HABITAT Deciduous and sometimes coniferous forest. Summer visitor to Britain.

FOOD AND HABITS Feeds on insects caught on the wing, and sometimes on the ground. Seldom hunts from the same perch twice. Breeds in hollows and may use nestboxes.

Spotted Flycatcher
Muscicapa striata

Adult

Catching insect

Juvenile

SIZE AND DESCRIPTION 14cm.
Back greyish-brown with pale underparts; close examination reveals a streaked forehead and faintly streaked upper breast. Bill and legs black, and black eye an obvious feature. Upright posture when perched.

VOICE Call a short shrill 'tzee'. Song quiet, simple and scratchy, often with soft trills.

HABITAT Open woodland and gardens throughout Europe in summer. Winters in Africa.

FOOD AND HABITS Flies up from perch to snatch flying insects, then returns to the same spot. Breeds in hollows or dense vegetation.

Stonechat
Saxicola torquata

SIZE AND DESCRIPTION 12cm. Male has a black head, white patch on sides of neck, white wingpatch and dark brown upperparts. Female duller with streaked brown upperparts.

VOICE Call a persistent 'tsak, tsak', like two stones being hit together; plaintive song.

HABITAT Coastal heaths, especially with gorse, rough hillside grazing and upland moors. Present all year in Britain, and locally common.

FOOD AND HABITS Diet is chiefly insects; also worms and spiders. Nests on the ground, often under the cover of a gorse bush.

Female

Juvenile

Male summer

Whinchat
Saxicola rubetra

Female/juvenile

Male summer

SIZE AND DESCRIPTION 13cm. Summer adult male speckled brown and fawn above, with a bold white eyestripe separating the crown from the dark cheek patch. Underparts pale orange. Female and juvenile paler and duller.

VOICE Call 'yu teck-teck'. Chirping song, often produced in song flight.

HABITAT Breeds in wet meadows, pastures and heaths across most of Europe. Winters in Africa.

FOOD AND HABITS Perches on raised spots such as telephone wires, from which it makes sallies to catch flying insects. Nest a grassy cup well concealed in a bush.

Wheatear
Oenanthe oenanthe

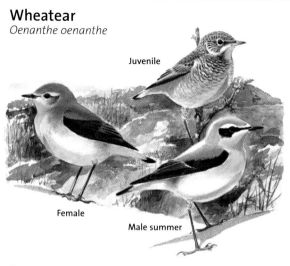

Juvenile

Female

Male summer

SIZE AND DESCRIPTION 15cm. Breeding male has a blue-grey back and black eye-mask, wings and lower tail; distinctive square white rump and upper tail visible in flight. Winter male is browner.

VOICE Call 'chack, chack'.

HABITAT Chiefly upland hills, pastures and cliffs; some lowland areas. Summer visitor to much of Europe; early spring migrant from March onwards. Winters in Africa.

FOOD AND HABITS Eats mostly insects. Nests on the ground in rabbit burrows, holes under stones and stone walls.

Nightingale
Luscinia megarhynchos

Juvenile

Size and description
16cm long. Both male
and female have
russet-brown plumage
with a rufous tail.
Skulking and secretive.
Voice Melodious and
loud song uttered by
day as well as late in
the evening and early
in the morning.
Habitat Lowland
deciduous woodland,

Adult

especially that containing coppice or dense bushy undergrowth.
Summer visitor to Europe except north. Breeds locally in southern
England. Winters in Africa.
Food and habits Eats mostly insects and worms; also fruits and berries.
Breeds in forests and thickets with dense undergrowth.

▶ **Similar species Bluethroat** (*L. svecica*)
13cm long. Breeding male's throat is blue,
divided from the whitish belly by black and
rufous breast bands. Female has a cream
throat bordered by black, sometimes with a
scattering of blue or rufous. Song is silvery
with mimicry, frequently delivered at night;
call a harsh 'track'. In Britain a very scarce
passage migrant mainly on east coast in
May or September.

Male
summer

Robin
Erithacus rubecula

Juvenile

Adult

SIZE AND DESCRIPTION
13cm. Familiar bird
with an orange-red
breast fringed with
pale grey, and a pale
wingbar. Juvenile has
a pale-spotted brown
breast, and a pale-
flecked head and back.

VOICE Call a repeated short
hard 'tic'; alarm call a thin sharp 'tsiih'. Song sweet and silvery, starting
high, then falling, then speeding up in clear notes.

HABITAT Woodland bird that breeds in gardens, parks and forest edges.
In winter, north European Robins migrate south-west to southern
Europe. Other populations are resident.

FOOD AND HABITS Feeds on berries and insects on the ground. Moves
over the ground by hopping vigorously. Nest a grassy cup well hidden
on or near the ground; may be in a cavity.

Black Redstart
Phoenicurus ochruros

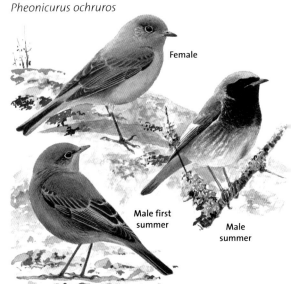

Female

Male first
summer

Male
summer

SIZE AND DESCRIPTION 14cm. Darker than Common Redstart. Breeding male slaty-black above with a black face and breast, and a white flash in the wing. Female duller brown. Reddish rump and tail.

VOICE Call a quiet 'tsip-tsip'. Song a short high-pitched warble punctuated by characteristic gravelly notes.

HABITAT Towns, urban sites and cliffs. Summer visitor to northern Europe. Rare breeder in south-east England.

FOOD AND HABITS Eats mainly insects. Constantly shivers tail. Often nests in wall cavities.

Common Redstart
Phoenicurus phoenicurus

SIZE AND DESCRIPTION 14cm. Male has a grey back, black face and throat, white forehead, and bright chestnut breast and tail. Female is a duller brown. Tail is waved up and down.

VOICE Calls 'hooeet' and 'kwee-tucc-tucc'. Song a squeaky warble.

HABITAT Usually deciduous upland woodland with mature trees for nesting. Occurs in much of Europe in summer. Winters in Africa.

FOOD AND HABITS Eats mainly insects; also worms, spiders and berries. Nests in a tree hollow.

Female

Male summer

Male first winter

Bearded Tit
Panurus biarmicus

Juvenile

Male

Female

Size and description 15cm. Tit-like with a plump body and very long and broad tail. Both sexes have rich orange-brown plumage, and male also has a grey head and black moustaches.

Voice Call like tiny bells, a ringing 'ching ching'. Song a softly chirping 'tship tship tshir'.

Habitat Favours reed beds. In Britain quite common in south-east England.

Food and habits Feeds on insects, and reed seeds in winter. Shuffles up and down reed stems. Builds an open nest of stems in reed beds.

Long-tailed Tit
Aegithalos caudatus

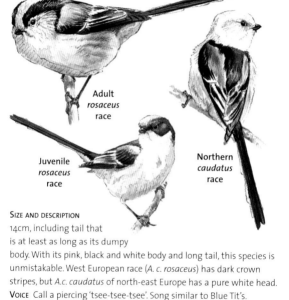

Adult
rosaceus
race

Juvenile
rosaceus
race

Northern
caudatus
race

SIZE AND DESCRIPTION
14cm, including tail that
is at least as long as its dumpy
body. With its pink, black and white body and long tail, this species is
unmistakable. West European race (*A. c. rosaceus*) has dark crown
stripes, but *A.c. caudatus* of north-east Europe has a pure white head.
VOICE Call a piercing 'tsee-tsee-tsee'. Song similar to Blue Tit's.
HABITAT Woods with bushy undergrowth, hedges and gardens
throughout most of Europe.
FOOD AND HABITS Feeds mainly on insects and small spiders, and is
increasingly visiting bird tables. Families form into flocks and move
through woods and hedges, often with other tits. Nest ball-shaped
and camouflaged with lichens, built in a branch fork.

Blue Tit
Cyanistes caeruleus

SIZE AND DESCRIPTION 12cm. Smaller than Great Tit and with a bright blue crown. Stripe down yellow breast less well-defined than Great Tit's. Tail and wings blue. Young birds have yellow cheeks, and blue parts are green.

Juveniles

VOICE Call a thin 'see-see'. Clear, ringing and high-pitched song.

HABITAT Mixed and deciduous woodland, parks and gardens. Found across Europe except Iceland and northern Norway.

FOOD AND HABITS Feeds on insects, spiders and other small animals, finding them on tree branches and sometimes in the corners of windows. Frequently visits bird tables in winter. Feeds in flocks of up to 30 in winter, often with other tit species. Nests in holes in trees, buildings or banks.

Adults

Great Tit
Parus major

Female

Male

Juvenile

SIZE AND DESCRIPTION 14cm. A black cap and black stripe starting at the bill give this bird a more ferocious expression than a Blue Tit's. Male's breast-stripe becomes broader than female's.

VOICE Rich and varied repertoire includes a metallic 'pink' and a repeated 'teacher-teacher'.

HABITAT Woodlands and gardens across Europe except far north. Many feeding in gardens in winter return to woods to feed in spring.

FOOD AND HABITS Feeds on seeds and fruits; also spiders and insect larvae in breeding season. Eats sunflower seeds, peanuts and fat at bird tables. Nest as Blue Tit's.

Coal Tit
Periparus ater

SIZE AND DESCRIPTION 11cm. Smaller than Great Tit with a proportionately larger head. Black head with white cheeks, and a white patch on the nape. Back grey and breast grey brown. Irish race (*P. a. hibernicus*) with pale yellow on cheeks, nape and underparts.

VOICE Most frequent call a triple 'tsee-tsee-tsee'. Song like a simpler and weaker Great Tit's song.

HABITAT Woodland and gardens across Europe except far north. Prefers coniferous trees.

FOOD AND HABITS Eats insects and seeds, particularly spruce cones in north. Nest as Blue Tit's.

Adult Irish
hibernicus
race

Adults

Marsh Tit
Poecile palustris

SIZE AND DESCRIPTION 12cm. Very similar to Willow Tit, with a large-headed and short-tailed appearance, but with a shiny black cap, smaller black bib and uniform wings.

VOICE Best distinguishing feature is call, 'pitchiuu'. Song a liquid bubbling sound.

HABITAT Mainly deciduous woodland, sometimes gardens, across much of central and western Europe.

FOOD AND HABITS Diet mainly insects, with seeds and berries, and beechmast, like other tits. Nests in tree holes, especially in alders and willows.

Adult

Adult

Willow Tit
Poecile montanus

Adult

SIZE AND DESCRIPTION 12cm. Plumage similar to Marsh Tit's, but Willow has a heavier neck, duller black crown, slightly larger bib and sometimes a pale patch on the closed wing.

VOICE Call variable, for example a low-pitched, nasal and down-slurred 'zur' or 'si-si-zur zur zur'. Song a melanchonic and bell-like 'tyu tyu tyu'.

HABITAT Forests, scrub and parks in Europe apart from south-west. In Britain resident in England, Wales and southern Scotland.

FOOD AND HABITS Feeds on insects, caterpillars and seeds. Nests in tree hollows, which it excavates itself. May visit birdfeeders.

Adult

▶ **SIMILAR SPECIES Crested Tit** (*Lophophanes cristatus*) 12cm long. Distinctive black-and-white head with a pointed crest. In Britain restricted in both range and habitat; breeds only in mature pine forests in the Scottish Highlands.

Nuthatch
Sitta europaea

Western Europe *caesia race*

Nuthatch descending tree

Northern Europe *europea race*

SIZE AND DESCRIPTION 14cm. Large head, no neck, short tail and heavy pointed bill. Back and head slate-grey with a long black eyestripe. Cheeks white, and breast and underparts rusty orange (darker in male). Flight similar to woodpecker's, but tail is rounded.

VOICE A loud strident 'hwitt' call. Song a repetitive 'peeu-peeu-peeu'.

HABITAT Mixed deciduous woods, parks and gardens with mature oaks from western Russia across Europe; absent from Ireland and Scotland.

FOOD AND HABITS Feeds on nuts, seeds and invertebrates, using bill to winkle insects out of bark crevices. Nests in a cavity, usually in a tree, with entrance plastered with mud to provide correct size.

Treecreeper
Certhia familiaris

SIZE AND DESCRIPTION 13cm. Mottled brown on back and white on underside, providing excellent camouflage against tree-trunks. Fine bill curves downwards. Long stiff tail helps bird balance in upright position against a trunk.

VOICE Call a loud and thin 'zzrreet'. Song is several scratchy notes ending in a thin trill.

HABITAT Almost all woodland, parks, gardens and orchards with old trees that have loose bark for nest-sites. Occurs throughout Europe except south.

FOOD AND HABITS Probes bark crevices for insects and small spiders. Nests in a crevice behind a flap of bark.

Adult

Juveniles

Golden Oriole
Oriolus oriolus

SIZE AND DESCRIPTION 24cm. Starling-sized bird with male plumage a striking yellow and black. Female golden-olive above with a yellow rump and yellow-tipped dark tail.

VOICE Call a harsh croaking 'khraayk'. Song a loud and beautiful flutey whistling, 'dode-lio'.

HABITAT Mature deciduous forests, poplar stands and parks across Europe except north and far west. Winters in Africa. In Britain a coastal migrant and rare breeder in East Anglia.

FOOD AND HABITS Feeds mainly on insects and fruits. Builds a hanging basket-shaped nest in a tree.

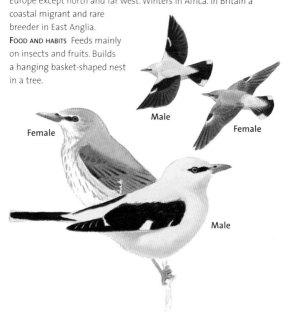

Male

Female

Female

Male

Great Grey Shrike *Lanius excubitor*

First
winter

Adult

Length 24cm. Pale
grey above, white below,
with a white eyestripe and long
tail with white edges. Hooked beak,
typical for shrikes. Sits prominently
on bushes and cables, from which it swoops
onto prey that includes insects, lizards, small rodents and birds.
Impales prey on sharp point like a thorn. Summer visitor to open
habitats with thickets in southern and eastern Europe. In Britain very
rare and mainly on east coast.

Red-backed Shrike *Lanius collurio*

Length 17cm. Male with a
rufous back, white-edged black
tail, grey crown and black
eyestripe. Female duller with a
dark brown smudge through
the eye and finely barred below.
Breeds in hedges and forest
edges, often near thorn bushes.
Winters in Africa. Extinct as
a breeding bird in Britain,
occurring only on coast in
small numbers on migration.

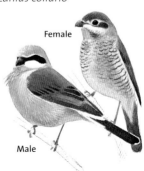

Female

Male

Jay
Garrulus glandarius

Adults

SIZE AND DESCRIPTION 34cm. Striking bird with a
pale eye, black moustaches and blue-and-black
wing-flash. Streaked feathers on forehead often
raised in crest. White rump obvious in flight.
VOICE Call a noisy screeching 'kscharch'.
HABITAT Forests and parks throughout Europe. Often best seen in
autumn when storing food.
FOOD AND HABITS Eats seeds, fruits, birds' eggs, nestlings and insects.
Buries acorns and beechnuts. Nest a shallow twiggy cup in the
fork of a tree.

Magpie
Pica pica

Juvenile

Adults

SIZE AND DESCRIPTION 44cm, of which 20–30cm is tail. Wings metallic blue-black, and long and round-tipped tail has a metallic-green sheen. Male larger than female, and tends to have a longer tail. Flight often a series of jerky flaps interspersed with swooping glides.

VOICE Noisy alarm call is a staccato rattle; also utters a variety of bisyllabic calls.

HABITAT Breeds around farms and villages, and in hedgerows. Increasingly common in urban areas. Occurs across Europe except Iceland, northernmost Scotland and far north of Norway.

FOOD AND HABITS Omnivorous; feeds on seeds, insects, carrion (often seen feeding on roadside casualties), nestlings and eggs. Nest a dome of twigs high in a tree.

Jackdaw
Corvus monedula

Adults

SIZE AND DESCRIPTION 33cm. Nape is grey and eye has a very pale iris. In flight, wingbeats are faster and deeper than Carrion Crow's. Struts as it walks. Flies in flocks almost as densely as pigeons.

VOICE Calls a metallic high-pitched 'kya' and 'chak'.

HABITAT Found in fields, woods, farmland and towns across Europe.

FOOD AND HABITS Feeds on invertebrates, eggs, nestlings and grains. Breeds in tree hollows or on ledges of buildings and cliffs, in pairs or small colonies.

Chough *Pyrrhocorax pyrrhocorax*

Length 39cm. Relatively slender crow with metallic black plumage, red legs and a slightly decurved red bill. Juvenile has an orange-yellow bill. 'Sneezing' call, 'keeach'. In Europe occurs in high mountain areas in south, and on coastal cliffs with adjoining meadows in west. Non-migratory resident in range. Scarce in Britain and found only on west coasts, although has recently recolonized Cornwall.

Adult

Hooded Crow *Corvus cornis*

Length 47cm. Grey underparts and back. Similar voice and habits to Carrion Crow, which it replaces in eastern and northern Europe. In Britain common in north-west Scotland and Ireland, and rare on east coast of England.

Adult

Carrion Crow
Corvus corone

Adult

SIZE AND DESCRIPTION 47cm. Totally black with a stout bill. Upper leg feathers neatly close-fitting. Juvenile much like adult, but duller.
VOICE Call a croaking 'krra-kra-kraa'.
HABITAT A wide variety of habitats, from coast to mountains and towns, throughout western and central Europe.
FOOD AND HABITS Omnivorous; feeds on carrion, nestlings and eggs, grain and insects. Not colonial. Nest a bulky twig structure high up in tree canopy.

Rook
Corvus frugilegus

Juvenile

Adults

SIZE AND DESCRIPTION 46cm. Large black bird with 'ragged trousered' appearance. Bare face patch makes the bill seem very long. Purple gloss to plumage. Juvenile has an all-dark face.

VOICE Calls coarse and nasal 'gaah' and 'grah".

HABITAT Farmland, both pasture and arable, with trees for nesting. Year-round resident in most of Europe, but summer visitor in north and winter visitor in south.

FOOD AND HABITS Eats mostly vegetable matter, seeds, roots, cereals and fruits; also a variety of animal food. Breeds in colonies, erecting bulky twig nests in trees.

Raven
Corvus corax

Adult

SIZE AND DESCRIPTION 61cm. Largest crow and largest passerine. Heavy head has shaggy throat feathers and a huge bill. In flight shows broad heavily fingered wings, a protruding head and a wedge-shaped tail.

VOICE Calls deep and croaking 'korrrk', 'klong' and repetitive 'korrp korrp korrp'.

HABITAT Coastal, forest and mountain areas year-round in much of Europe, though largely absent from central Europe. In Britain found only in west and Ireland.

FOOD AND HABITS Feeds on carrion, as well as small mammals, birds, molluscs and vegetable matter. Builds a bulky nest from twigs in a tree or on a rocky ledge.

Starling
Sturnus vulgaris

Juvenile moulting into first-winter plumage

Adult winter

Adult summer

SIZE AND DESCRIPTION 21cm. Short tail and neck, upright stance, pink legs, white spots and metallic green shine. Non-breeding plumage has clear pale spots, which are reduced in breeding male. Breeding male also has a yellow bill; bill otherwise blackish. In flight, has an arrowhead profile. Flocks fly in tight formation. Juvenile grey-brown.

VOICE Versatile mimic of other birds. Calls are creaky twitters, chirps, clicks and whistles.

HABITAT Widespread throughout Europe in all habitats, particularly human settlements.

FOOD AND HABITS Eats berries, seeds and fruits. Breeds in holes. Outside breeding season roosts in huge flocks in city buildings and trees.

House Sparrow
Passer domesticus

Male summer

SIZE AND DESCRIPTION
15cm. Male has a grey cap and grey breast, with an extensive black throat-patch. Female has a pale brown cap and buff eyestripe. Wings of both sexes have small white wingbars.

VOICE Monotonous chirps; song a sequence of 'tshilp' and 'tshurrp' calls.

Female

HABITAT Completely linked to humans. Found in towns, villages and farmland near human habitation. Common but declining.

FOOD AND HABITS Omnivorous; feeds on seeds and insects, as well as bread and other food left by humans. Breeds mostly on buildings. In winter flocks feed in fields.

Male winter

Tree Sparrow
Passer montanus

Juvenile

Adults

SIZE AND DESCRIPTION

13cm. Sexes look similar.
Distinguished from male House
Sparrow by chestnut crown and nape, white cheeks, small neat black
bib and black spot behind the eye.

VOICE Song more musical than House Sparrow's.

HABITAT Farmland and suburbs, but not a town bird. In winter flocks
to feed in stubble fields with finches and buntings. Widespread and
common in some parts of Europe. Increasingly scarce in Britain.

FOOD AND HABITS Feeds mainly on weed seeds and corn; also insects
and spiders. Nests in holes in trees.

Chaffinch
Fringilla coelebs

Male summer

Female

Male winter

SIZE AND DESCRIPTION 15cm. In winter blue-grey of head and pink of breast in male are subdued. Female similar to female House Sparrow. Two white bars on each wing.

VOICE Call a sharp 'pink'; flight call a softer 'yupp'. Song a loud ringing trill that becomes lower, ends in a flourish and is then repeated.

HABITAT Breeds in all types of woodland, and in parks and gardens. Flocks form in autumn. British Chaffinches are resident, but birds from elsewhere in Europe may winter in Britain.

FOOD AND HABITS Eats fruits and seeds, and also insects during breeding season. Nest a neat cup of moss, grass and feathers bound with spiders' webs, usually built in a tree fork.

Brambling
Fringilla montifringilla

SIZE AND DESCRIPTION 15cm. In all plumages has an orange breast and a large white patch on the rump and lower back. Breeding male has a black head and bill. Female always has a brown-grey head.

VOICE Call a rasping 'zwee-ik'. Song simple and monotonous, like a distant saw, 'rrrrrhoo'.

HABITAT Breeds in north European forests. Occurs widely as a winter visitor in beech forests south to Mediterranean.

FOOD AND HABITS Feeds on beechmast, seeds and berries, and insects in summer. Nest a deep cup of moss, grass and hair, lined with feathers and wool, and decorated with bark and lichen; usually built in a tree fork.

Male winter

Female winter

Hawfinch
Coccothraustes coccothraustes

Male summer

Female summer

Juvenile

SIZE AND DESCRIPTION 18cm. Big head, huge bill and short tail. Bill is blue-black in summer, becoming brown in winter. Male's flight feathers are black, female's secondaries are grey. In flight, white wingbars are visible.

VOICE Call a sharp 'tic'. Song a soft series of 'zih' and 'zri' notes.

HABITAT Deciduous and mixed woodland. More widespread and confiding on the Continent than in Britain.

FOOD AND HABITS Feeds on seeds, cherry stones and nuts. Nest a bulky twig platform high in tree canopy.

Bullfinch
Pyrrhula pyrrhula

Male

Juvenile

Female

SIZE AND DESCRIPTION
16cm. Compact bull-
necked finch with a
black cap. Male has a
rosy red breast, grey back, white rump and black tail. Female has a
pale brown breast. Juvenile has a grey-brown head and breast. White
wingbars of both sexes show in flight, which is fast and undulating.
VOICE Call a soft and sad fluted whistle.
HABITAT Mixed woodland, parks, large gardens and churchyards. Feeds
in orchards and gardens. Widespread and resident throughout Europe
except far south.
FOOD AND HABITS Feeds on buds and seeds, and insects in breeding
season. Nest a shallow platform of twigs built in a shrub.

Linnet
Carduelis cannabina

Female

Male summer

SIZE AND DESCRIPTION 13cm. Breeding male has a crimson forehead and breast, and a chestnut mantle. Winter male resembles female.

VOICE Canary-like song is a pleasant twitter consisting of chirping and rolling sounds, sung from the top of a bush.

HABITAT Open fields with bushes and waste ground. Farmland and coasts in winter. Widespread throughout most of Europe.

FOOD AND HABITS Mostly eats seeds and arable weeds. Often breeds in loose colonies. Nest a grassy cup well hidden in a shrub. Common but declining due to changes in agricultural practices.

▼ **SIMILAR SPECIES Twite** (*C. flavirostris*). 13cm long. Highland version of Linnet. Sexes very similar; male may have a faint pinkish-tinged rump. Bill yellow in non-breeding birds, blackish in breeding phase. In Britain

Adult winter

Adult summer

breeds on moorlands of Scottish Highlands, northern England and north Wales. In winter found near coast in Scotland and eastern England. Forms large flocks outside the breeding season.

Lesser Redpoll
Carduelis caberet

Mealy
Redpoll

Male
summer

Female

SIZE AND DESCRIPTION
12cm. Greyish-brown and
dark-streaked with a red
forehead and small black bib;
small broad bill. Adult male
has a red upper breast. Wings
have faint wingbars.
Juveniles lack red head.
VOICE Flight call a hard
metallic 'chet-chet-chet'.
HABITAT Breeds in forests (especially birch) and on heaths from Britain
to southern Scandinavia and western central Europe.
FOOD AND HABITS Feeds in flocks, searching among tips of birch trees for
seeds. Nest a neat cup high in a tree.
SIMILAR SPECIES Mealy Redpoll (*C. flammea*), 13cm. Paler and less brown
than Lesser Redpoll. Rare winter visitor to north and east of Britain.

Goldfinch
Carduelis carduelis

Adults

SIZE AND DESCRIPTION
13cm. Red face,
white cheeks and
throat, black cap
and black-and-gold
wings. In flight
wings show broad golden bands, and white
rump and black tail are visible. Sexes alike,
but juvenile has a brown-streaked head.
VOICE Cheerful trisyllabic 'tickelitt' call.
Song a series of rapid trills and twitters.
HABITAT Open lowland woodland, heaths,
orchards and gardens in most of Europe.
FOOD AND HABITS Eats seeds and berries.
Favours teasels and thistle heads. Nest
made of hair and rootlets; positioned
high in canopy.

Juvenile

Greenfinch
Carduelis chloris

Male

Female

SIZE AND DESCRIPTION 15cm. Summer male olive-green, merging into grey-green on the face, wings and flanks; bright yellow wing feathers on sides of tail. Female and juvenile paler with streaking, stronger in latter. Bouncing undulating flight.

VOICE Flight call a sharp 'burrurrup'. Song a wheezy sequence of twitters and whistles.

HABITAT Breeds in woodland edges, open woodland, parks, gardens and farmland with hedges. Year round in much of Europe.

FOOD AND HABITS Eats seeds and berries, and some insects during breeding season. Visits garden bird tables. Nest a cup of grass, twigs and moss in a tree or bush.

Siskin
Carduelis spinus

Juvenile

Male

Female

SIZE AND DESCRIPTION
12cm. Dark-streaked
greenish-yellow plumage.
Male yellower than female,
with a black cap and bib.
Wingbars in both sexes are
yellow, and male's tail has
yellow patches on either side.
Tail deeply notched. Flight flitting and uneven.
VOICE Flight call either a descending 'tilu' or a rising 'tlui'; twittery
and trilling song.
HABITAT Coniferous and mixed forests in winter in much of Europe.
FOOD AND HABITS Seeds of trees. Nest a cup of twigs high up in a tree,
usually a conifer.

Serin
Serinus serinus

Female

Male

SIZE AND DESCRIPTION 11cm. Smallest finch, with a tiny conical bill. Male yellow-green with dark streaks, a bright yellow head and breast, and a yellow rump; breast becomes brighter as it wears. Female rather duller.

VOICE Song has a jingling quality.

HABITAT Gardens, parks and churchyards. Rare in Britain, breeding very occasionally, mostly in Devon, Dorset and East Anglia; common in central and southern Europe.

FOOD AND HABITS Mostly eats plant seeds, including alder and birch seeds. Nest a tiny cup of grass and moss high up in a tree.

Common Crossbill
Loxia curvirostra

SIZE AND DESCRIPTION 16cm.
Sturdy, with a crossed
bill-tip adapted to feed
on spruce cones. Adult
male an unmistakable
red all over. Female
smooth dull green or
almost brown. Juvenile
streaked; young male
with less red than adult.
VOICE Call a liquid 'chip
chip chip'. Song similar to
Greenfinch's, with chirping
and trilling.
HABITAT Fir and spruce forests
in much of Europe. Also
breeds in winter in some
parts of range.
FOOD AND HABITS Feeds on pine
seeds. Nest a flat twiggy
platform high up in a tree.
▶ SIMILAR SPECIES Scottish
Crossbill (*L. scotica*) 16.5cm
long. Very similar to Common
Crossbill, but with a slightly
longer bill. Confined to
Caledonian pine forest in
northern Scotland.

Female

Male

Male

Corn Bunting
Emberiza calandra

Adults

SIZE AND DESCRIPTION 18cm. Large plain bunting that is brown with dark streaks. No white markings.

VOICE Distinctive monotonous jangling song is high-pitched, likened to keys being jingled.

HABITAT Farmland, arable land and grassland with bushes and hedges across much of Europe except far north.

FOOD AND HABITS Mostly eats seeds, corn, fruits and other vegetable matter; also insects and earthworms. Very sedentary. Sings from a prominent perch. Nest a grassy cup well hidden on the ground.

Snow Bunting *Plectrophenax nivalis*

Length 17cm. Male becomes progressively whiter with the approach of spring. Breeds on tundra. Winters on fields and dunes around North Sea and northern Black Sea. In Britain mainly a winter visitor to coast, especially in north and east.

Male summer

Male winter

Lapland Bunting *Calcarius lapponicus*

Length 15cm. Breeding male has a strikingly marked head; head much paler in female and non-breeding birds. Breeds on northern tundra. Winters on dunes and fields around North Sea and northern Black Sea. Scarce visitor to Britain, principally to coastal locations in autumn and sometimes spring.

Female

Male

Cirl Bunting *Emberiza cirlus*

Female

Length 15cm. Male has a striking black-and-yellow face pattern. Female paler and less boldly patterned. Breeds in southern and south-western Europe. Very rare in Britain, breeding in a few rural areas in south-west England.

Male

Yellowhammer
Emberiza citrinella

Juvenile

Male

Female

SIZE AND DESCRIPTION 16cm. Male has a vivid yellow head, brown-streaked back and chestnut rump. Female is duller.

VOICE Song a jingling phrase on one note, 'a little bit of bread and no cheese'.

HABITAT Arable farmland grassland with banks or hedges. In winter flocks to feed in stubble fields and farmyards. Widespread in much of Europe including Britain, but declining.

FOOD AND HABITS Feeds on grasses, seeds and fruits; also insects. Nest a cup of grass low in a shrub.

Reed Bunting
Emberiza schoeniclus

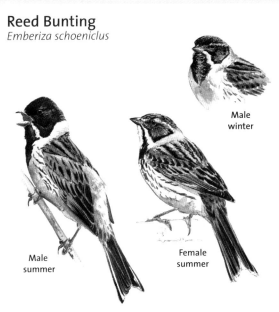

Male
winter

Male
summer

Female
summer

SIZE AND DESCRIPTION 15cm. Summer male has a rich brown back
streaked darker, grey-brown rump, blackish tail with white outer
feathers and whitish upperparts. Crown and face are black, with a
white collar running into white moustachial streaks; throat and upper
breast also black. Winter male, female and juvenile less boldly marked.
VOICE Call 'tsee-you'. Song a repetitive 'tsit tsit tsrit tsrelitt'.
HABITAT Marshes, scrub and farmland in much of Europe.
FOOD AND HABITS Feeds mainly on seeds. Often perches on reed stems
or telegraph wires. Nest a grassy cup concealed low in vegetation.

Index